Land and Water for Recreation

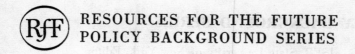

RESOURCES FOR THE FUTURE
POLICY BACKGROUND SERIES

Land and Water for Recreation

OPPORTUNITIES, PROBLEMS, AND POLICIES

MARION CLAWSON

RAND McNALLY & COMPANY · CHICAGO

POLICY BACKGROUND SERIES

WEBB S. FISER, State University of New York, Editor

333.78
C617*l*

Printed in U.S.A. by Rand McNally & Company
Library of Congress Catalogue Card Number 63:1936

Preface

This book is written for the intelligent interested nonspecialist. It seeks to present the major facts and issues about outdoor recreation, both for the present and for the future. It omits details of interest primarily to the specialist. Supporting evidence is generally not included.

This book draws heavily on a number of research studies on outdoor recreation made by the author and his associates at Resources for the Future. Some of this material is included in *Land for the Future*, by Marion Clawson, R. Burnell Held, and C. H. Stoddard (Johns Hopkins, 1960) ; other parts are included in more technical reports, most of which are now unfortunately no longer in print. Persons interested in this field should give particular attention to the report of the Outdoor Recreation Resources Review Commission, a special governmental organization established in 1959. Its final report, *Outdoor Recreation for America*, published in early 1962, is available from the United States Government Printing Office; 27 rather detailed study reports have been published or are planned for publication.

It is believed that this book may be used for general reading assignments in advanced high school courses, as reading material for basic college courses, and with adult education classes. It should also be of value and interest to citizen groups, such as the League of Women Voters, and to various conservation and recreation groups.

The discussion in this book seeks to place outdoor recreation accurately within the national framework—economic, cultural, and political. Interest in outdoor recreation has mounted rapidly since the war; shortages of suitably developed areas have become apparent in many places; and extravagant statements about the role of out-door recreation have been made all too frequently. Hopefully, the information in this book will help to set this activity in a more accurate relationship to other activities in the nation.

CONTENTS

LIST OF TABLES

LIST OF FIGURES

1

LEISURE AND RECREATION
IN MODERN LIFE

THE AGE OF MASS LEISURE IS UPON US, IN THE
United States. In past ages, and even today in most parts of the
world, very few people have had any real leisure. All their efforts
were or are required to produce food, clothing, shelter, and the other
necessities of life. Only the very rich or the privileged classes have
had much leisure. Our rising productivity has enabled us to increase
our material standard of living while at the same time making it
possible to have leisure time for play, relaxation, enjoyment, and
personal self-fulfillment. Some leisure is used for outdoor recreation,
but most is used for other purposes.

One distinction must be made at the outset: leisure is not the
same as idleness. In the past, and in many primitive societies today,
a large proportion of the people are idle during a large part of the

1

year. Lacking adequate income for even the basic necessities, they have neither money, energy, nor ideas for use of this time as purposeful, chosen leisure. On the other hand, many Americans find themselves busier, with more commitments for their time, during leisure than during work. Leisure is time not spent on the job or in the basic elements of personal living—time available for uses one wants to make of it, "choosing time." As such, it is comparable to the discretionary income that people have after food, housing, and other basic necessities are cared for. One can overcommit either his money or his time budget.

Over the centuries, the use of leisure has shaped civilizations and cultures as much as has work. In ancient times, it was the few scholars and religious leaders, not required to labor for their sustenance, who advanced learning in their time and for us, in directions and to a degree which have determined the nature of our present-day society. In the great period of the Middle Ages, it was the few scholars, often in monasteries or universities, who kept learning alive and added to it. Today, it is the scientist in the laboratory, the student at school, the citizen reading or listening to the radio or looking at TV, who is largely forming the society of the future.

CHANGING LIFE PATTERNS

Major changes have taken place in typical life patterns of Americans in the past several decades. A striking and easily measured change has been the increase in life expectancy; at birth in 1900, the average life expectancy of a boy baby was 48 years, in 1950 it was 65½ years, and by 2000 it may well be 73 to 75 years. Much of this gain in life expectancy has come through saving a much larger proportion of the lives of newly born babies, but our senior citizens are also living to older ages. Great-grandparents are becoming as common today as grandparents were a century ago.

The typical man has three major life stages: growing up, productive employment, and retirement. The increase in life expectancy has made possible a lengthening of each of these life stages. A generation ago, most boys began work after finishing elementary school; today, most finish high school or college; and a generation from now, the completion of college will be the usual stage for beginning work. The working years have lengthened out, too; and yet the average years in retirement have doubled in the past generation and are likely to increase further in the next. Although adequate data are lacking for women, something similar has happened to them also. In the case of women today and in the future, a relatively large proportion will enter the labor force at eighteen or twenty years of age, work for a few years, leave the labor force to bear children, but re-enter it at forty-five years or so, after their children are in school or grown, and then retire again at perhaps sixty-two years.

Another effect of the longer life expectancy is the changed age distribution of our total population. In particular, the number and proportion of people sixty-five years and older has risen greatly in the past; in the future, the number in this age bracket will continue to rise, although the proportion may not rise much further if birth rates, and hence numbers of young people, continue high.

Still another basic population change has been the massive shift from farm to city. At the time of the First World War, the United States was half rural, half urban; today it is two-thirds urban, and by 2000 it may be four-fifths or five-sixths urban. Moreover, the size of the average city is growing, too, so that people are living in more intensely urban environments all the time. This is true even though the trend in recent decades has been toward the suburb; the suburb is a basic part of the large city, quite different from the small city and town of the past. For various reasons, rural people participate actively in outdoor recreation much less than do city people. It may be that, with the rural environment all around them, they feel the need of special excursions to park and forest less than do city dwellers; it often has been that they could not afford a trip to a special outdoor recreation area. At any rate, almost all studies agree

3

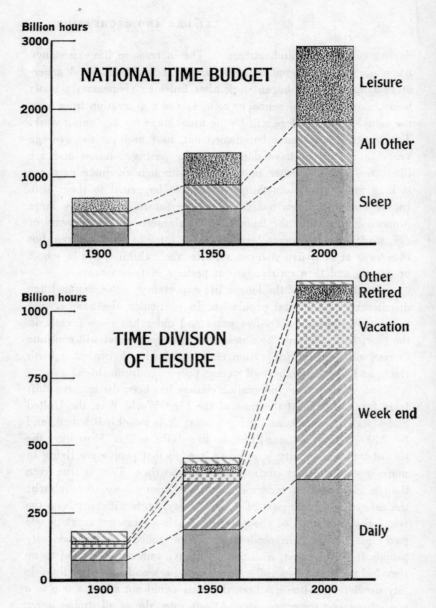

Figure 1. By the year 2000 the total population may well spend 38 per cent of its time in leisure activities.

that rural people patronize public outdoor recreation areas proportionately less than do city people.

Those people who are in the labor force have had increased leisure over the past several decades. At one time, six- and even seven-day workweeks were common; today, few workweeks (except for self-employed people, and often not for them) are over five days. Once, workdays were ten and even twelve hours; today, they are only rarely over eight hours. At the end of the First World War, the steel industry—which is typical of round-the-clock continuous operations—was on a seven-day, twelve-hour daily workweek. Today, the 40-hour workweek is the norm—some jobs are a little longer, some shorter, with the average only slightly below 40 hours. Another great change of the past few years—since the Second World War—has been the rise of the paid vacation. Almost all union contracts now provide for some paid vacation, whereas a generation ago it was only some of the professional classes who had such vacations. Moreover, the length of the typical paid vacation has been increasing, from one to two, to three, and even to four, weeks.

In 1900, the 76 million people in the total population had 667 billion hours (365 days of 24 hours each) for the whole year; of this, about 26½ per cent could be classed as leisure—time left over after work, sleep, school, housekeeping, and personal care (Figure 1). By 1950, total hours for the entire population had doubled and the proportion of leisure hours (by the same definition) had risen to 34 per cent. By 2000, total hours will more than double again, and the proportion in leisure (again by the same definition) will rise to 38 per cent. A rising percentage of a doubling total obviously means a greatly increasing total of leisure hours for the whole nation: 177 billion hours in 1900, 453 billion in 1950, and 1,113 billion in 2000. About half of the increase in total leisure hours from 1900 to 1950, and from 1950 to 2000, was due to an increased population; the rest of the increase in leisure was due to more hours per person. The greatest relative increases will be in the paid vacation hours and in the retired leisure time.

TIME AND ORDER IN
MODERN AMERICAN LIFE

One consequence of the vast economic and social changes of the past decades has been to make us modern Americans intensely "time minded." We watch clocks, not so much in the sense of hoping for the workday to pass so that we will be free, as in the sense of ordering nearly all our activities by the clock. We rise at a predetermined time, brought to our attention by the alarm clock; we eat, ride to work, begin our day's work, take our coffee break, eat our lunch, quit work, ride home, eat our dinner, look at TV, and retire, all according to the clock. Indeed, given the mass society and mass production processes which have made possible our productive, varied, rich society, we could scarcely do otherwise. A factory production line or an office could not function if workers reported and left as they chose. Radio and television programs are scheduled at definite times; while this makes for a degree of regimentation, it also opens up an opportunity for millions of people that would be impossible if everyone insisted upon his favorite program at a time of his own choosing.

In this time-oriented modern life, the hours of both work and leisure are socially determined to a very large extent. If a particular job is organized on a 40-hour workweek, the individual cannot decide he wishes to work only 39 hours or that he wants to work 41. He cannot say, "I prefer an extra hour's work and an extra hour's income rather than an extra hour's leisure," because that choice is not open to him. If work hours are too onerous, he may decide to change jobs; but this often means loss of accumulated skills and knowledge, and of seniority as well, so that he may be most reluctant to take this step. If hours of work are too short and pay too low, he may decide to get a second or even a third job—about 4 per cent of all workers hold more than one job. But this presents its problems, too.

The social determination of time applies to leisure also. As individuals, we have some leisure each day, some over the week end, and some during vacation, in a pattern largely determined by our employers, our fellow workers, and society in general. If, as seems probable, we have more leisure time in the future than we have today, its form and timing will also be socially, rather than individually, determined.

OUTDOOR RECREATION AS A USE OF LEISURE

One outlet, but only one, for the available leisure time is outdoor recreation. In later chapters, we shall trace briefly some of the history of outdoor recreation, its present extent, and its probable future growth. Suffice it to say at this point that attendance at every major kind of outdoor recreation area has risen steadily and rapidly for the past several decades, as far as we have information to measure it. At the appropriate season, over the week end or on holiday, when the weather is good, Americans pour out by the millions to beach, lake, mountain, and other areas, for a myriad of activities.

But we must also keep some perspective about the role of outdoor recreation in the whole leisure picture. As nearly as we can estimate, only about 3 or 4 per cent of all leisure time is used for outdoor recreation activity. This superficially very low figure results in part because about 40 per cent of all leisure is daily leisure, after work or after school, during which it is often difficult for many people to get to an outdoor recreation area; and much leisure is at seasons when outdoor recreation is not attractive to the average person. Even if one excludes daily leisure, outdoor recreation occupies only about 7 per cent of the remaining leisure. The proportion of leisure spent for outdoor recreation has risen greatly in recent decades, as nearly as we can estimate, and presumably will continue to do so in the future.

Outdoor recreation can be, and for millions of Americans is, a wholesome and personally rewarding way of using some of the available leisure. Its role will probably increase in the future. But it seems most unlikely that it will ever be the major use of the average person's free time. Some of his time is in small pieces daily, when it is not convenient to get outside for recreation; some is in times of the year when he will prefer indoor activities; but in any event, some people simply will not wish to use more than a limited amount of time for outdoor recreation. We cannot pack everyone off to Yellowstone or Grand Canyon national parks, nor even to a state park 50 miles away, nor yet even to a neighborhood park three blocks away. These are all important recreation and leisure time activities for most people, but they can scarcely absorb all leisure time.

Many social scientists have been much concerned with mass leisure. While leisure can be a major means of self-achievement, especially in today's highly organized society, yet it is also true that leisure can be wasted or worse. "The Devil finds mischief for idle hands to do." Mere idleness, without constructive outlet, is likely to have bad consequences for society and for the individual. Outdoor recreation can be one important use of leisure, with beneficial results to individual and society alike; but it cannot be the complete answer to the larger problem of the constructive use of leisure time.

The timing and size of pieces of leisure are as important, as far as outdoor recreation is concerned, as is the total annual amount of leisure. If future gains in leisure come primarily by means of longer and more nearly universal paid vacations, then this will have a major impact upon the use of outdoor recreation areas best suited to vacation use—mountain, seashore, and similar relatively distant areas. Should an increasing percentage of the labor force work only four days a week, this would permit use of the added day as the "chore" day, and the family would increasingly turn to week-end recreation trips and experiences. On the other hand, should the hours of work per day decrease, this would lead to an increased demand for golf courses, tennis courts, and other types of areas close enough to residential areas that workers could use them in the extra hour or even half hour. These are but some of the examples of how the timing of leisure affects outdoor recreation.

8

NEED AND DEMAND FOR OUTDOOR RECREATION

Some recreation specialists, many social workers, and others emphasize the role that outdoor recreation plays in a physically and emotionally healthy individual. According to this view, the normal person needs some outdoor recreation as a relief from the tensions of job and living in the modern urban world, and that without this outdoor recreation experience there is grave danger of ill health, physical or emotional. This view is rather widely held, in varying degrees of intensity. We doubt its accuracy seriously; at the least, we have seen no convincing evidence that outdoor recreation is essential to either physical or emotional health. We suspect there are as many emotionally ill-adjusted wandering through the woods or lying on the beaches as there are cooped up in the apartment before the TV set; and that, conversely, there are as many well-adjusted who never go near the outdoors as who do. But these may be only our prejudices, contrasting with the prejudices of those who insist upon the essentiality of the outdoor experiences.

Regardless of how one views *need* for outdoor recreation, there can be no question that a major part of the total population *demands* it, given a free choice. Millions of Americans spend not only part of their leisure but also part of their available income to enjoy outdoor recreation in one or more forms. They are willing to spend money for this purpose in preference to spending it for some other use. Since income for most people does not permit unlimited consumption of everything, this means that outdoor recreation is preferred to some alternative use of the same income. Moreover, since the rate of growth in use of outdoor recreation areas is greater than the rate of growth of most alternative uses of consumer incomes, we may well deduce that the demand is shifting toward a greater appreciation of outdoor recreation. If opportunities for outdoor recreation exist and are relatively good in the future, then we may expect that increasing numbers of people will choose to spend more of their

9

time and money upon this activity than upon alternative uses or activities.

Demand for outdoor recreation is more accurately and quantitatively measured than the need for outdoor recreation can be measured—or at least, so it seems to an economist. We can observe how many people come to particular areas, and how much they are willing to spend to do so. These represent free choices on their part; free choice by consumers is a basic strength of the whole American economy and society. While there are problems in forecasting what the consumer will do, especially over the longer-run future, yet this problem for outdoor recreation is not seriously different from the similar problem for any consumer good. In Chapter II, we shall try to suggest some of the factors that have been responsible for the great past rise in outdoor recreation activity, and to make some estimates of possible future increases in demand.

PUBLIC AND PRIVATE ACTIVITIES IN OUTDOOR RECREATION

Most outdoor recreation in the United States takes place on publicly owned and provided areas, including water bodies open to the public. Some individuals own their own outdoor recreation places, but in most instances these people also use public areas. The family which owns a cottage at the beach depends upon the publicly available sand and water for much of its enjoyment, for instance. This situation varies considerably by kinds of activities. Hunting, fishing, camping, picnicking, hiking, and other extensive land use activities are largely upon public lands and waters. Recreation activities involving intensive use of limited areas are more likely to be on privately owned facilities, though often on group rather than individually owned ones.

There are several reasons for the dominance of the publicly owned areas. For one thing, the minimum adequate area for most outdoor recreation activities is simply too large and too expensive for any but the very richest people to have their own; for another,

10

such areas ordinarily have ample capacity for far more people than the members of a single family. It is not only the cost of owning such areas, but also the costs of minimum upkeep and service, that may be decisive. For many kinds of outdoor activities, supervision or instruction is also needed, and this, too, can usually be provided most economically on a larger scale than the single family (even than for the "extended" family).

At any rate, public provision of outdoor recreation areas is a widely accepted aspect of American life. The role of private lands and waters in outdoor recreation may be larger in the future, as we shall discuss in more detail in later chapters, but outdoor recreation seems likely to continue to be carried out largely on publicly provided areas.

POLICY ISSUES

Several major issues of national policy arise out of the foregoing considerations. Perhaps the basic one, and hardest to define and understand is: what sort of culture do the people of the United States want? We are frequently characterized by critical groups in other countries as intensely materialistic; yet in many respects we are highly humanistic, for it is the values of the individual which are most highly prized and protected. But, shall we give primary emphasis to physical output of goods, such as millions of tons of steel, millions of autos, and the like? Or shall we equally or more highly value intellectual attainments? Perhaps an even more basic question is: how far and how consciously as a nation should we debate and decide such questions, and how far should we allow decisions to be made as incident to labor-management bargaining and in the marketplace for commodities? How could a nation such as ours, with its dispersed decision-making, its lack of a single powerful planning center, carry out any common decision as to the nature of society? In spite of the difficulties, do we wish to let the major decisions go by default?

11

These broader issues find more specific expression in terms of the role of leisure and of recreation. How far should the general public be concerned with working hours per week in typical employments? Is the relative proportion between work and leisure wholly a matter for the persons and business firms concerned, or is there a general public interest also? This matter will almost surely come to a head in a specific issue between some major labor union and some large industrial concern in the next few years. Several major unions are even now seeking to shorten average working hours as a means of spreading employment among more workers. Do we care whether average workweeks are shortened, and whether they are reduced by giving longer paid vacations, or working fewer days per week, or by working fewer hours per day? The consequences for outdoor recreation, as we shall emphasize again and again, would be very great.

Another special phase of this problem concerns the older people. Do we regard their retirement, even on a retirement pension which is adequate for their needs, as a satisfactory solution to their problems? Retirement is a busy and satisfying period of life for many people, but for all too many others it is a period of frustration. Moreover, can society afford to lose the productivity still present in a large proportion of the people who reach compulsory retirement age? Could some means be found whereby such people could still be active, perhaps on a reduced scale, and not necessarily for large monetary rewards, but in ways that would be both personally satisfying and socially productive?

As we have noted, in our opinion outdoor recreation can fill only one place in the total leisure picture—an important place, but still a minor one in terms of total time. But others may doubt this conclusion. Just how important can outdoor recreation be, and should we strive to make it a much larger component of the total leisure situation of the future?

2

OUTDOOR RECREATION
ACTIVITIES:
PAST AND PRESENT

OUTDOOR RECREATION AREAS AND ACTIVITIES
are numerous and varied, and they must be grouped into broad
categories for more ready understanding and comparison (Figure 2).

At one end of the scale are the *user-oriented* areas and activities.
These are characterized by their close proximity to the residences of
their users. City parks of all kinds are major examples of this type.
Such areas have only modest requirements for natural resources—a
relatively few acres, some of which are moderately well drained and
reasonably level, will suffice for a playground or city park, for instance. But location of such areas is highly important; they must be
near enough to where people live that they can be used in the time
available—usually after school or after work—or they are unusable.
Playgrounds must ordinarily be within a half mile of where children

13

14

Figure 2. Kinds of outdoor recreation areas in relation to location of population.

live in order to be useful, for instance. Areas of this type are intensively used, with hundreds or thousands of visits per acre annually. On this type of outdoor area, activities tend to dominate, area characteristics being less important.

Intermediate outdoor recreation areas are located farther from the users' homes, but usually within a distance where they can be used readily for all-day outings. This means within two hours' travel distance, or less, which in turn means less than 100 miles distance. Within such a range, this type of area normally chooses the most attractive sites. Larger individual sites are usually chosen than for the first type, although some beach and swimming areas are comparatively small. Some of these areas may be for general outdoor recreation activities, with rather more emphasis upon activities than upon natural qualities of the site. For others, emphasis may shift to the site qualities as such—an excellent forest with its manifold interests, for example. In the last two decades or so, particular interest has focused upon water-based recreation, and the most popular outdoor areas of the intermediate type usually include some water. In some instances, the water may be dominant and the surrounding area more or less incidental. Artificial water bodies—reservoirs built primarily for purposes other than recreation, or artificial lakes primarily for recreation—may do very well for this kind of outdoor recreation.

A third major type of outdoor recreation area is the *resource-based*. Here, primary emphasis is upon the natural or human qualities of the site, much less emphasis upon the activities at the site, and almost none on the location factor. One common type of such area is the national park; here the emphasis is upon the unique natural characteristics of the area, which give it national significance. As a matter of fact, such areas mostly lie at some distance from where most people live, hence fairly long travel is necessary to reach them. This in turn means that they are visited primarily during vacations. Other examples of resource-based areas are the outstanding historic sites, where early or present-day man has carried on some activity which gives the spot special significance. Such sites are often

15

small, only a few acres or less in extent. Some are within large cities—Independence Hall in Philadelphia, for example. Among the natural areas, the degree of access may vary greatly, from many favorite spots in the most popular national parks which are accessible by auto, to the more remote wilderness areas which are accessible only by pack-train, on foot, or by canoe.

There are innumerable variations in kinds of areas within this broad grouping, and many kinds of outdoor recreation activities, especially on the closer and more intensively used areas. Each appeals to certain groups in the population, or to the same people at different times and in different ways. To some extent, one kind of area is competitive with another: on a Sunday, a man may play golf at a user-oriented golf course, or he may take his family for a day's outing at an intermediate type of area. Far more important than the competitive relationships are the complementary ones, however. That is, a family active in outdoor recreation will wish to avail itself several times during the year of varied activities on the parks and playgrounds within and near the city in which it lives; will go for a day's trip to a state park or federal reservoir a few times during the year; and during its vacation will go fishing or camping in a distant mountain or lake area, for instance. Although precise data are lacking, it appears that people who use one kind of area and undertake one kind of activity liberally, also use other kinds of areas and undertake other kinds of activities liberally. Experience at one tends more to generate a taste for others than to replace them, it appears. The fact that one kind of area can be enjoyed best during one kind of leisure, and other areas during other kinds of leisure, is a further important fact in the complementarity of kinds of areas and activities.

CITY PARKS

Public parks in cities in the United States are only about a hundred years old. The early New England town typically had a common area in its center, used at first as a cow pasture, but later gradually developing into a public park. Philadelphia purchased a park of 24 acres in 1828, and in 1853 New York City began the purchase of land for Central Park, but these experiences were exceptional until well after the Civil War. By 1880, 66 out of the 103 cities with 1950 populations of 100,000 or over had one or more parks. Many of these were small, many cities had but one or a few such parks, and they were not developed as we know them now; nevertheless, a good beginning had been made. Parks in those early years were primarily open unimproved space, for walking and informal sports.

The concept of publicly provided and publicly supervised playgrounds began only about the turn of the century. By that time, the idea of city parks had begun to have wider acceptance. As nearly as our imperfect statistics permit us to tell, it seems that the areas of city parks expanded relatively faster from 1880 to perhaps 1940 than did the populations of the same cities. This is contrary to a common impression of shrinking play and recreation area in cities in those decades. While these formally established public areas were thus expanding, privately owned vacant land, often consisting of a few open lots in a settled area, was gradually disappearing. Thus, an increase in publicly available and often improved areas was off-set, more or less, by a decrease in open unimproved areas.

Since reasonably reliable statistics first became available, about 1910, every measure of city park management shows greatly increased intensity of management and use (Figure 3). The number of supervised playgrounds has mounted rather steadily, at a fairly high rate; the number of recreation buildings and indoor centers has been fewer but has also increased, perhaps even more rapidly; and the number of paid recreation leaders has increased most rapidly and most steadily of all. The only significant exception to these generalizations is during the period from 1930 to 1935, when the severe depression forced many cities to curtail their services of all kinds, including recreation services. We lack reliable statistics of actual use of city parks and playgrounds. Most of them are open to access by anyone, with no means of keeping attendance records. But all the indications of facilities and services provided, plus the usual

17

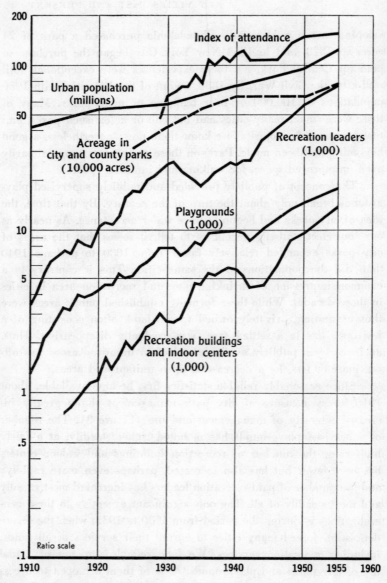

Figure 3. Some measures of growth in availability and use of city and county parks and recreation facilities, 1910–1955.

accounts of heavy demand for all services available, suggest that usage has mounted rapidly over the past several decades.

Although the area of city parks and recreation areas expanded relatively rapidly during the latter part of the nineteenth century and the first decades of the twentieth century, this does not mean that their area was adequate to meet the need at any time. "Adequacy" is not easily defined, yet recreation specialists have come up with certain rough rules of thumb which are often used; one such standard is that a city should have one acre of city park or playground for each 100 of its population, plus another acre of larger city or regional park on the outskirts or margin of the city for more extensive types of recreation use. Even this area is not adequate unless the separate tracts are well located with respect to the need for them, and unless they are well planned, well developed, and well managed. In 1940, about a fourth of cities with any parks met this standard, and some exceeded it considerably; but an equal number of cities, about half of them the smaller ones, reported they had no parks or playgrounds at all; and a full half of all cities, almost all smaller ones, failed to report on parks and must be presumed to have had but very few of them. In 1956, the total area of city and county parks was about ¾ million acres; an adequate area, by the above standards, would have been 2 million acres.

Since 1940, the relationship between park and recreation area and total population has been a less happy one. Area within the legal boundaries of the larger cities has expanded about as population has grown; but, when the population of the surrounding suburbs has been added to that of the central city, the area has lagged seriously. In a great many urban areas, the suburbs have failed to add land to meet their needs, trying to rely on the older parks of the central city. The latter have become increasingly less adequate to meet their old demands and these new ones also.

Cities of all types and sizes have difficulty providing adequate park and recreation area for their residents. Part of the difficulty is financial, but only part; parks and recreation must compete with many other essential public services for the limited tax revenues available. But there is also a problem of suitable open areas available for public purchase and use. In the older and densely settled parts of the larger cities, it would be simply impossible to have enough park and recreation land to meet these standards, regardless of cost. For instance, land to meet this standard for the population of Manhattan would exceed the area of the island itself. Intensive land use for all purposes and high land values require that available recreation and park areas be used intensively there. Just as land for office buildings or for residential purposes is used intensively in the central part of larger cities, so must the limited area of recreation land also be used very intensively. Some kinds of recreation activities can be carried out on these limited land areas; other kinds must be enjoyed only on larger areas some distance from the city center.

The growing suburbs, which have so dominated the urban scene since the Second World War, experience a different kind of difficulty in providing enough park and recreation land. Here, there is no shortage of potential land, nor are costs forbiddingly high. Instead, the problem is to reserve the land for public use before it gets built on for private use. The typical growing suburb is desperately short of revenue to meet its most essential demands for schools, streets, fire houses, and minimum continuing public services. There has been a tendency to postpone acquisition of park and recreation land, often with the consequence that desirable land is not available when needed.

In an effort to meet some of these problems, the federal government in 1961, by amendment to housing legislation, provided for federal grants-in-aid to states, counties, cities, and special governmental districts, to procure open space in and around cities. These grants may be 20 per cent of the cost of land purchased by one city, or 30 per cent of the cost when the land is part of a metropolitan land acquisition program; in either case, the land purchase must fit into a long-range program of park and recreation development for the urban area.

City and other local park and recreation areas can be visited by most users with little or no cash cost. Their nearby location insures

20

this situation. One might thereby suppose that such parks were used primarily by low income people who could not afford to visit more distant parks where the necessary travel costs were larger. But, in general, this is not true. For one thing, all income classes use city and local park and recreation areas to a large extent because they can be visited in the time available for such activities—the after work and after school time, referred to above. But there is often a serious disparity in the availability of such park and recreation areas and facilities *within* cities. The densely populated parts of the city—often decadent or outright slums—frequently have the most inadequate areas. Children and adults from these areas often must play in the streets, seek indoor recreation activities—for which facilities are often equally inadequate—or just plain do without. People from the very highest income levels may not use public park and recreation areas extensively—our data are inadequate, but this seems to be true; in part, they can substitute their own home or private club areas. City parks and recreation areas are most valuable to and most used by the great middle classes of our urban population.

STATE PARKS

State parks are a more recent phenomenon than are city parks. As late as 1928, only 26 states had any parks; only nine of these provided annual appropriations for park management on any significant scale; and over 80 per cent of the total area was in New York alone (Figure 4). As early as 1883, New York prohibited any further sale of state-owned land; it actually owned nearly 800,000 acres at that time in the Adirondacks and Catskills. In 1894, by constitutional provision, New York decreed that these lands should be kept forever wild, with no tree cutting under any circumstances. Substantial areas of private land have been purchased since that date, until today these reserves contain $2\frac{1}{4}$ million acres. In California, the federal government gave part of what is now Yosemite National Park to the state in 1864 as a state park; in 1906, the state of California

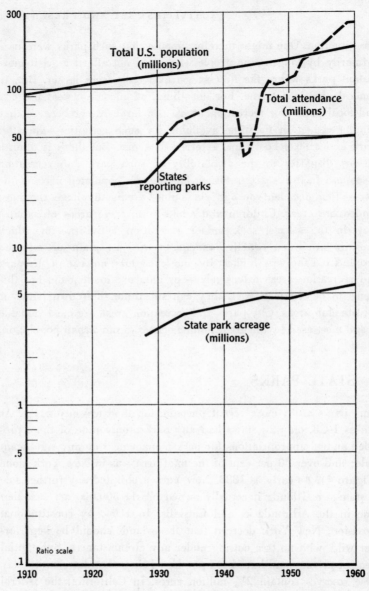

Figure 4. Since 1930 the use of state parks has grown at a rate far exceeding the rate of increase in population.

gave the land back to the United States, largely because the state had demonstrated its incapability to manage the park properly. In 1885, New York established Niagara Falls state park. But these early efforts are significant largely because they were forerunners of the present-day system of state parks.

The state parks of the country really owe their origin to some of the federal New Deal programs. During the 1930's, when unemployment reached alarming proportions, various federal programs were undertaken to provide jobs to otherwise unemployed men and women. Some of the more important, as far as outdoor recreation is concerned, were the Civilian Conservation Corps, under which several hundred thousand young men were enlisted for specific work programs; the Public Works Administration, under which major public works were undertaken; and the Works Progress Administration, under which smaller-scale, often largely hand-labor, programs were carried out. Funds for these programs came from the federal government, and were either disbursed by it or transferred to states for specific agreed-upon projects. States were so eager to get projects under these programs, to employ local people, that they embarked upon major park and recreation projects. By 1940, almost all states had some form of state park system; the area outside the big New York reserves increased fourfold between 1930 and 1940. Roads were built into the new parks, sometimes dams were built to establish artificial lakes, camp and picnic areas were developed, and other improvements were made. As late as 1950 many state parks were primarily dependent upon improvements built in this way.

The federal programs of this period gave major assistance to state parks in two other ways. Some grant funds were provided for state park and recreation planning, which enabled many states to develop plans which had never previously had any. Federal funds were also used to buy marginal and submarginal farm lands, which were later turned over to the states for parks.

Since the end of the war, the use of state parks has risen enormously. This has been especially true for state parks with water bodies, either natural or artificial, where the various water sports can be enjoyed. For some years after the war, state parks increased in area slowly, available funds for management and improvement were often inadequate, and these parks rather quickly became seriously crowded in many instances. A remarkable development of recent years has been the proposal and adoption of state park plans in a few of the larger and more progressive states, under which substantial funds are raised by bonds, and which have provided help to counties and cities as well as the expansion of the state park systems. Massachusetts, New York, New Jersey, and Wisconsin have been notable in this regard. Other states, such as Michigan, have not resorted to bond financing but have developed major state park programs.

By 1954, the general pattern of state parks had rather clearly evolved. In that year, there were on the average slightly more than three acres of state parks per 100 of population. However, this is a most misleading "average"; only seven states exceeded it, and the other 41 states then existing fell short of the average. Many states in all major regions fell below one acre per 100 persons. Nearly half of all state parks were less than 100 acres each; many of these closely resemble the larger city parks, but are simply located a few miles outside the nearest city and are managed by the state rather than by a city. At the other end of the scale, eight state parks of 50,000 acres each, located in five states, have 64 per cent of the total state park acreage.

About 95 per cent of all use of state parks is on a single-day basis; only about 5 per cent is for overnight. The latter often resembles the use of national forests and national parks, which we discuss later. The day-use character of most state parks means they must be located where visitors can get to them and return home, and still have adequate time for enjoyment at the park, all within one day. As we noted earlier, this usually means a park location within 100 miles of where people live. Attendance at state parks tends to be highly concentrated on week ends, especially on Sunday; and tends further to be heaviest during the afternoons. As a result, many state parks are severely crowded for a few hours each week, and used to less than capacity at other times during the week.

24

State parks have one other characteristic of great importance for recreation planning: their number can be increased greatly, for they often can be made from land and water resources rather easily available. The greater flexibility in location of these parks, as contrasted to city parks, is a major advantage in this regard. While state parks should include scenic and enjoyable areas, their natural resource requirements are not nearly as demanding as those of national parks, which we consider later. Rolling land, not highly valuable either for farming or forestry, can often be developed into quite attractive parks. Rather low dams, of fixed overflow outlets, can create artificial lakes in small stream valleys which in the course of a few years take on the appearance of natural lakes. Natural or planted forests provide scenic areas for hiking, riding, nature observation, and the like. Camping, picnicking, swimming beach, and boating areas can be developed frequently. All of these combine to provide attractive and satisfying areas—not natural wonders like Grand Canyon, but pleasant areas to relax and play in, whose convenient location goes a long way to offset any resource mediocrity.

FEDERAL RESERVOIRS USED FOR RECREATION

A large number of reservoirs built by federal agencies for various purposes have significant recreation values. Most of these reservoirs have been built in the past thirty years, and their greatest use for recreation has taken place since the Second World War. The Bureau of Reclamation began building storage reservoirs for irrigation, and later for hydroelectric power production and flood control, soon after it was created in 1902. By 1955, 140 such reservoirs had been built, all in the western half of the United States. Management of the reservoirs and surrounding lands for recreation has been turned over to other federal agencies, such as the Forest Service when the reservoir was within national forests, or to state and local recreation agencies, whenever such an agency existed that could undertake this task. The Corps of Engineers has constructed flood abatement works

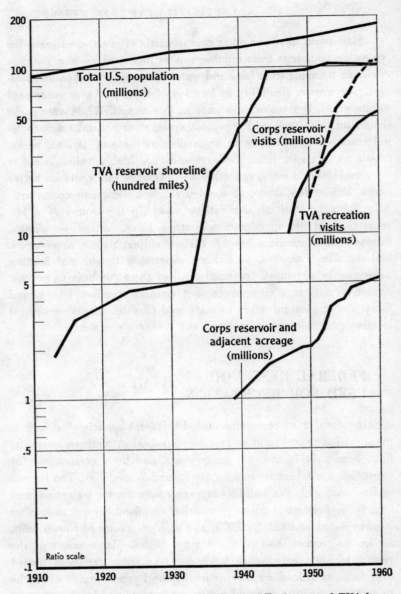

Figure 5. As the reservoirs built by the Corps of Engineers and TVA have grown in size and number, their recreational use has more than kept pace.

26

and navigation improvement projects for more than a hundred years, but it has relied upon major dams and reservoirs only during the past 30 years or so. It now has built over 150 dams, the reservoirs of which have important recreational values. Like the Bureau of Reclamation, it tries to induce states and local agencies to administer the recreation areas and programs around these reservoirs. A third major federal agency, the Tennessee Valley Authority, has about 30 major dams and reservoirs, which also have a great recreation use. As with the other two agencies, it turns most of the recreation program over to states and local governments.

The location, size, operating program, and other characteristics of these federal reservoirs are determined by water management problems and considerations other than recreation. In a few cases, recreation possibilities may have been a major factor in the planning and operation of the project, but for the most part recreation is wholly incidental to other purposes. No provision existed in federal law, until very recently, whereby recreational values could be included in the economic valuation of such projects, nor any means whereby recreationists could help repay the federal expenditures on such projects. Naturally, therefore, recreation had to be a secondary consideration for them. In spite of this, the bodies of water so created have been highly popular, especially in regions of the country lacking large natural bodies of water.

Many kinds of recreation activities are carried out on, in, or near water. Some are essentially shore activities—picnicking, camping, swimming; others are carried out away from shore. Some, like trolling for fish, are best in quiet water; others involve relatively active use of the water, as do water skiing and power boating. Conflicts arise among water recreationists over the best use of the water body. There has been an enormous rise in water-based outdoor recreation since the war (Figure 5). The use of outboard motors and boats has increased greatly in recent years, aided in part by the more common use of the boat trailer, which enables the boat owner to store his boat at home and to use it on several lakes during the course of a season. The horsepower of motors has also increased greatly, permitting the use of a larger boat or the attainment of higher speeds, or both. Water skiing, once nearly unknown, has become very popular. Skin diving and other underwater sports have also become very popular, in large part because of the development of relatively low cost equipment for these purposes. All in all, a near-revolution in use of water for recreation has occurred in the past two decades.

Some of the most difficult problems of water management and development that the nation will face in the next generation involve the use of water for recreation. Our growing population and industrialization each mean a vastly increased volume and variety of wastes dumped into streams and other water bodies. Formerly, most wastes were natural; these tended to decompose readily and thus permitted the streams to purify themselves over time or distance. But wastes are increasingly coming to consist of various synthetic chemicals, such as detergents, which decay very slowly or hardly at all. These wastes can be taken out of domestic and industrial water, at some expense but as needed; but to preserve streams, lakes, and other water bodies in a pure enough state for recreation means that such wastes must largely be kept out of them. This may be both difficult and expensive. It may also be difficult to say whether or not the necessary waste disposal programs "pay" or not; aesthetic considerations may be as important as economic ones.

MAJOR PUBLICLY OWNED
RESOURCE-BASED AREAS

The federal government today owns a third of our national area, when Alaska is included, or a fifth of it if Alaska is excluded. This is the remainder of a once much more extensive area, for more than two-thirds of the nation has been owned by the federal government at one time or another. When the new nation was first formed after the Revolution, those states owning extensive "western" lands outside their boundaries surrendered their claims to such land to the new national government. As additional territory was added—by the Louisiana Purchase, by treaty after the war with Mexico, by treaty with Great Britain over the Pacific Northwest, by purchase of Alaska from Russia, and in other ways—the land acquired in each case became the property of the federal government. The major part of this land was sold, given away, or granted to individuals, states, railroad companies, and others.

But a movement to keep part of these federal lands permanently in public ownership developed during the last quarter of the nineteenth century. The first major reservation was that of Yellowstone National Park, in 1872; the first major system of permanent federal landownership was that of the forest reserves, now called national forests, which began in 1891. These were expanded to almost their present extent by 1910. National parks have been added periodically ever since the first one; federal wildlife refuges have been established to protect rare species and migratory waterfowl; and grazing districts have been organized since 1934 to bring the remaining federal lands into definite management units (Figure 6).

Recreation, in the sense of city park recreation, is not the primary purpose, or indeed any purpose at all, of these federal lands. But their preservation for public use, as natural, scenic, scientific, and historical areas, is a major purpose. For the national parks (and national monuments and other units of this system), this is the sole purpose. For the national forests and many other management units, recreation is a major purpose in a program of multiple-use management. When first established, many of these areas of federal land were comparatively isolated from population centers, and hence were difficult and relatively expensive to visit. Moreover, these were decades when all forms of outdoor recreation were severely limited by income, travel, leisure, and other considerations. With the passing years, however, the various kinds of federal lands have become increasingly popular. Use of them has increased about 10 per cent annually for as long a period as we have records. The only major exception to this statement was the war period, when travel restrictions reduced attendance at them. Visits have usually increased,

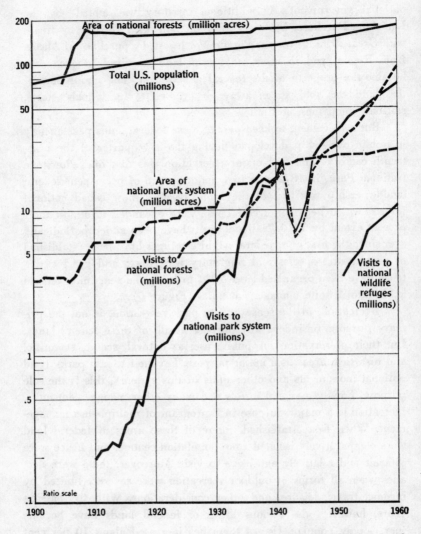

Figure 6. Growth in visits to the national park system, national forests, and national wildlife refuges, compared with growth in acreage and population, 1900–1960.

though at a slower rate, even during periods of depression and unemployment.

These federal resource-based outdoor recreation areas exhibit certain important characteristics in their use. If one looks only at their total area and their total number of visits, usage is extensive, less than one visit annually per acre. However, by far the greater part of the use—perhaps as much as 95 per cent—of the federal lands takes place on a relatively small part—perhaps as little as 5 per cent—of the total land area. On the remaining larger part of the federal areas, recreation use is very light indeed.

Most of the federal resource-based outdoor recreation areas lie a considerable distance from where the great majority of Americans live. Visits to such areas thus require considerable travel, on the average; they also require considerable time, thus largely limiting use to vacation periods; and they also involve costs, at least modestly high, which make it impossible for the lowest income classes to enjoy these areas. More than half the visitors to Grand Canyon National Park came more than 1,000 miles from their homes to the park, for instance; and the trip of which this park visit was a part cost the average party over $500. This is an unusually long distance and high cost, though by no means the extreme; obviously, the very geography of the situation severely limits the use of the areas to certain income classes and to certain time periods.

The qualifications of the national park system are severely limited. Parks must be outstanding areas, of national importance. Most qualifying areas are now in federal ownership. Some additional ones have been proposed for acquisition. In addition to public reluctance to authorize further federal landownership, even for this purpose, there are many difficulties in expanding this system, the most serious of which is lack of really outstanding undisturbed tracts of sufficient size. Comparatively modest additions to the national park system and still smaller additions to other federal land holdings seem probable.

If additions to area in the future will be limited, use of these outstanding recreation areas is likely to continue to increase. The past rate of growth, roughly approximating 10 per cent annually, shows no signs of leveling off. A growth rate of this magnitude, if long continued, leads to truly astronomical figures. Present-day use of the major national parks is 20, 30, or even 40 times what it was 40 years ago. Yellowstone National Park had less than 100,000 visitors in 1920, but has 1½ million annually today, for instance. If present growth rates continue unmodified, use 40 years from now will be 20, 30, or 40 times what it is today. How can we possibly crowd 20 or 25 million visitors into and out of Yellowstone in a three-month season? It is extremely difficult to see how use intensities of this magnitude can be accommodated at all; and certainly they would profoundly change the character of the recreation experience in these areas. The human foot, if there are enough of them, can as effectively destroy important qualities of the landscape as can the bulldozer. The management problem of these areas is a subject to which we shall return in Chapter IV.

A BRIEF SUMMARY OF
OUTDOOR RECREATION ACTIVITIES

The foregoing discussion can be summarized most briefly and quantitatively in a statistical table (Table 1). Municipal parks are the smallest, relative to other types; have by far the heaviest total use, or use per acre (in excess of 1,500 visits annually) and per person (six or more annually). Resource-based areas are the largest in total and in area primarily for recreation; have the lightest total use, lightest use per acre (less than one visit per acre annually), and least per person (only about one annually). Intermediate areas are actually intermediate in total area, in use per acre (about 40 visits annually), and in use per person (about two visits annually). In addition, the average person got in about one day of fishing and somewhat less than one day of hunting each year.

On this basis, an average person in the United States had about eleven days' (or major parts of days) outdoor recreation on public

TABLE 1
AREA AND ATTENDANCE
MAJOR TYPES OF OUTDOOR RECREATION AREAS

| Major Type of Outdoor Recreation | Kind of Areas Representative of Each Type | Present Area (million acres) | | Attendance | |
		Total	Primarily for Recreation	1960 or 1961 (million)[1]	Average Annual Percentage Increase in Postwar Years
1. User-oriented	municipal parks[2]	0.7	0.7	1,000 plus	4
2. Resource-based	national park system	25.7	25.7	79	8
	national forests	181.5	14.9	93	10
	wildlife refuges	28.3	28.3	11	12
3. Intermediate	state parks	5.6	5.6	258	10
	TVA reservoirs	.67	.67	53	15
	Corps of Engineers reservoirs	5.3	3.9	121[3]	28

[1] Most recent year of record; data are in terms of visits, except for wildlife refuges and TVA reservoirs, which are in terms of visitor days.
[2] All these data are for 1955.
[3] 1961.

areas or in hunting and fishing annually: six or more visits (often less than a full day each) in local parks, about two days in intermediate areas, about one day on a more distant resource-based area, and about two days of fishing and hunting. There is some overlap between the latter, if on public land, and the former categories; but there are also some omissions, especially because the data on use of municipal parks are so sketchy. Some of the visits to local areas are after school or after work; some visits to intermediate areas are on week ends; but nearly all visits to resource-based areas are during vacations. As we noted in Chapter I, these various outdoor recreation activities occupied only a small part of the total available leisure.

33

There is, of course, very great variation among individuals in the use of outdoor recreation—many enjoyed it not at all, others did so far beyond the average. But the average figures do give some measure of where recreation fits in the national life.

FACTORS UNDERLYING GROWTH IN RECREATION ACTIVITY

What accounts for this relatively rapid, long-sustained growth in use of outdoor recreation? A number of factors may have entered in, but four seem dominant: population changes, income changes, improvement in travel facilities, and increased leisure (Figure 7).

Among the population changes, one obvious factor has been the growth in total population. From 106 million in 1920, by 1960 we had grown to 179 million; and in another 40 years, by 2000, we shall have grown to somewhere between 300 and 350 million. But other population changes are also important. For instance, the proportion of the population living in cities has also increased, as we noted in Chapter I. Urban people use recreation, or at least use public recreation areas, more than do rural people. The population has also grown older, with more people in retirement; and it will continue in this direction.

Real income per capita has risen greatly, if somewhat irregularly, throughout our national history. Its changes have sometimes been masked by price changes and by periodic booms and depressions. Over a long period, however, real income per capita has risen slightly faster than total population—each has increased at somewhat less than 2 per cent annually for the past several decades. Average disposable income per person today is roughly $2,000; the best prospect is that it will about double by 2000. Moreover, as incomes rise a larger proportion is available above the strict necessities of life—the "discretionary" income which is of such concern to marketing men. A larger percentage of available income is spent for recreation when income is high than when it is low. Thus, when average incomes rise, total expenditures for recreation rise in two ways: more total money available, a larger proportion spent for recreation.

As we have noted, almost all recreation involves some travel, and sometimes includes a good deal. Fifty years ago, relatively few people

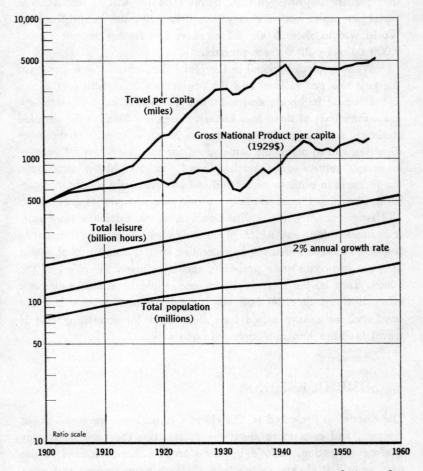

Figure 7. Four important factors explain the continuing growth in outdoor recreation activities since 1900: more people have enjoyed more leisure, higher income, and greatly improved travel facilities.

35

owned autos, roads were poor, and a trip to a park 100 miles away was a major undertaking. Today, the overwhelming majority of people own cars, roads are excellent, and trips to a park 100 miles away can be undertaken as part of a day's outing. It seems probable that further improvements in travel facilities will occur. Average travel per capita has risen from less than 500 miles before the First World War to about 6,000 miles today; and further increases up to 9,000 miles by 2000 seem probable.

We have already noted in Chapter I the increases in leisure over the past two generations, and the prospects for the future.

It would be highly desirable, but it is nearly impossible, to separate the effects of these four factors. When one looks at the detailed statistics, it becomes apparent that each was changing in the same direction and at about the same speed for the past 40 or 50 years—an annual rate of something less than 2 per cent. At the same time, the increase in outdoor recreation use was relatively steady at something like 10 per cent annually—a rate several times as great. With all changes steadily in one direction, and at somewhat the same rate, it is impossible to say which of the four basic factors was primarily responsible for the changes in recreation use. It seems probable that all were involved; quite probably, each reinforced the effect of the others. That is, the changes in income would have had much less effect if travel facilities had not improved and if leisure had not increased; or leisure would have been used for something else if travel facilities had not improved; and so on.

SOME QUESTIONS

The discussion presented in this chapter raises some questions about the past, and even more about the future. Has the basic desire for outdoor recreation, as held by the average citizen, changed in the past, or will it change in the future? With more income and more leisure, and better travel facilities, the average man today partakes of more outdoor recreation than did his father, and especially more than did his grandfather. But, given the same income and leisure, would the latter have used outdoor recreation to the same degree? Or has there been a change in basic tastes and desires? Whatever may be the facts as to the past, what about the future? Will basic attitudes remain constant, subject only to changing social and economic conditions, or will the attitudes toward recreation themselves change? We think it impossible to answer these questions unhesitatingly, either for past or for future; but the answers make a great deal of difference, in actual park administration. Lacking experience with each generation under a sharply different set of conditions, we cannot be sure how it would behave.

A closely related set of questions are: have factors other than population changes, increases in income, increases in leisure, and better travel facilities been strongly influential in the past? Or may they be in the future? We have noted that it is nearly impossible to disentangle the separate effects of four factors, each changing in a closely similar way. By the same token, it would be impossible to measure the effect of some fifth or sixth factor, if it too were changing similarly. The author judges that no other factors have been or will be of equal importance with those discussed; but it is wholly possible that this judgment is wrong.

When will future growth rates for use of various outdoor recreation areas level off? Past rates simply cannot continue indefinitely, for at some point this would require more time than exists. For instance, if postwar rates in use of Corps of Engineers reservoir areas continued unchanged to 2000, by that time every man, woman, and child in the whole population would be using a Corps reservoir 2,500 days annually—a rather excessive rate, by any standards! Even before carried to such extremes, limitations of time would surely become important; the total number of days at resource-based areas would probably not exceed 30 to 50 annually except for the most avid addicts, and would average perhaps less than half of this, even with much higher incomes and much longer paid vacations than at present. Limitations of interest might well become serious long before limitations of time, strictly speaking. With all the time and money one might wish, even trout fishing may pall after a while. Absolute limits to outdoor recreation may be far above present average enjoyment—so far as not to seem a relevant consideration. But, as the more enthusiastic outdoorsmen approach that limit, their use will reach a plateau and exercise a dampening effect on the rise in average use. Such a time will surely come, but there is little in the historical record to indicate whether it will be ten years from now, or 30 years hence; and whether it will be at a level of outdoor use four times or ten times the present.

3

WHO AND HOW MANY USE OUTDOOR RECREATION?

WHO ARE THE PEOPLE WHO USE OUTDOOR RECRE-
ation facilities? Do they have any special characteristics, or is it possible to deduce use of outdoor recreation from data on age, income,
and other characteristics of the population? Are the numbers who
use outdoor recreation in general or who use a specific facility or
area in any way related to population characteristics, including
spatial distribution of population? What are the roles of costs, distance, and accessibility, in determining use of outdoor facilities?

These are some of the questions to which this chapter is directed. We seek first to establish some general principles, then to
illustrate them in a few specific situations, and finally to raise some
policy questions which the available data seem to suggest.

39

ANTICIPATION

In anticipation of an outdoor recreation experience, a family plans where it will go and what it will do, and buys equipment and supplies

RECOLLECTION

and this in turn leads to planning for next trip.

Back home again, the family recalls its recreation experience, often with great pleasure. Memories may be an important part of the whole experience

TRAVEL TO

In order to reach the outdoor recreation area of its choice, a family must travel. Considerable expense is involved in such travel, and often as much time is consumed in travel as later on the site. Travel is often not as pleasurable as experience on the site

TRAVEL BACK

When the activities at the site are through, the family must travel back to its home. Often tired, frequently in a hurry, sometimes broke, the family is in a different mood than when it travelled in the opposite direction

ON SITE

When it arrives at the recreation site, the family may engage in many activities. Bodies of water are especially valued for outdoor recreation. The activities at the site generally provide the basic purpose for the whole experience, even when they occupy less than half the time and require less than half the total expense

Figure 8. Phases of the whole outdoor recreation experience.

NATURE OF THE
OUTDOOR RECREATION EXPERIENCE

First of all, we need to consider more carefully just what it is that we seek to measure and to describe. In Chapter II, we considered numbers of visits to various kinds of outdoor recreation areas; this is a common approach to this matter. It tends to focus on the outdoor area itself, and the activities carried on there. But this is only a part of the whole situation; a better understanding results if we consider the nature of the recreation experience more carefully.

An outdoor recreation experience consists of five more or less clearly separate phases: anticipation, travel to, on site, travel back, and recollection (Figure 8). Each of these is present in every outdoor recreation experience, although their relative importance may vary greatly. Let us consider each in a little more detail.

Anticipation is the planning stage of an outdoor recreation experience. It takes place in the recreationist's home town, usually in his own home. This is when he decides where to go, when, with what equipment, for what specific activities, which members of the family will go, how long they will stay, how much they can afford to spend, and all the rest of it. The planning may be careful and methodical, based upon ample accurate data; or it may be impressionistic, uninformed, mere wishful thinking; or it may be something intermediate. This is perhaps the most important stage of the whole experience, for what takes place later all has its origins here—even though plans may not work out exactly. As we shall show in Chapter VI, this is also the phase of the whole experience where more than half of all the costs are incurred. This is the phase where special equipment is bought, where one stocks up with gasoline and groceries.

Travel to the actual recreation site is also necessary, unless one has the necessary facilities in his own back yard. This travel may be short, as to a neighborhood playground or a city park; or it may be extremely long, as when one visits a national park across the country; or it may be intermediate in length. For most outdoor recreation activities, travel to the site requires an appreciable proportion of the total time spent on the whole experience; often as much time is spent in travel as later is actually spent on the site. Considerable costs are also involved in this travel. We lack definite information as to how such travel is regarded by the average outdoor recreationist. Some must regard it as pleasurable, for many people report sightseeing and travel as the chief attraction in their outdoor recreation experiences. For others, travel may be unattractive but a necessary part of getting where they wish to go.

On site experiences are those commonly thought of in connection with outdoor recreation. They run a gamut of specific activities—organized sports of all kinds, hunting and fishing, camping and picnicking, the variety of water sports, all sorts of specialized activities such as rock climbing and cave exploration, and much just plain resting and loafing. For some purposes, it is possible to group all these activities together, as outdoor recreation, as we are mostly doing in this book; but, to the park or playground administrator as well as to the participant, each separate activity presents its own requirements, problems, and rewards. For the general outdoor recreation experience, participation is often on a family basis, and a variety of activities to appeal to different age and sex groups is essential.

Travel back is in some ways the counterpart of travel to the area, but it may have important differences. The routes need not be the same, nor the time spent, nor even the money spent. Perhaps most important of all, the recreationist and his family may approach this travel in a different spirit than they did travel to the site. We know very little about travel either way, and still less about differences according to the direction of the travel.

Recollection is the last of the major phases. Like the first, it takes place primarily in the recreationist's home town, in his home or office or in the homes of his friends. It may be supplemented by pictures taken on the trip, or by souvenirs brought back. It may bear little relationship to what actually happened—the fish get bigger, the mosquitoes get more numerous, or the athletic exploits get more outstanding. But no small part of the payoff of the whole ex-perience takes place here; it is the memories that people carry with them that determine whether they will go back. Recollection of one experience gradually merges with planning for the next.

In considering outdoor recreation of any kind, these five phases form a package—a package of costs which must be considered, a package of results which must be balanced against the costs. No one element of cost can be considered independently of the others. It does not help if the entrance fee is low or even free, if other costs are high; people are likely to remember and to gripe about having to pay an unreasonable price for a cup of coffee. Magnificent scenery in the park may long be remembered, but so may dirty rest rooms at service stations en route. All aspects of the whole experience add together to provide a range and variety of pleasurable experi-ences; all costs of the whole experience also add together, and must be more than offset by the advantages if the user is to repeat the experience.

In considering ways to improve the total recreation experience, attention should be directed to each phase, not merely to the on-site phase. In the author's judgment, the greatest opportunity for im-provement of the outdoor recreation experience lies in the two travel phases. Our modern highways are mostly fast, comfortable, and safe; but the average traveller has little idea of what he is seeing or what it means. By signs and maps, we have taught him how to go from one city to another, or from one point on a map to another. But we have never been much concerned with what he saw or what he thought about what he saw. The new interstate superhighways are particularly bad in this regard; one can travel them with almost nothing to indicate what state, region, or locality he is in—New England, Middle West, South, and Far West all look alike. It should be possible to devise practical attractive means of involving the traveller's mind as well as his body. Well-written little leaflets, small roadside radio broadcasts that could be picked up only for a radius of a few miles, recorded tapes or strips that could be played back within the car, and perhaps other devices could inform those travel-

43

lers who want to be informed, about geology, geography, forests, agriculture, industry, history, government, and other aspects of the local countryside through which they were travelling. By making this voluntary in some form, it would not offend those who prefer the latest songs or baseball games on the radio, and it might delight those who travel in hopes of learning something. Programs of this sort might be undertaken by government agencies, either federal, state, or local; or by private firms—there seems no more reason why they should not be undertaken privately than that the provision of road maps should be largely a private activity; or by a combination of public research and writing with private business provision of the necessary service. The typical park or recreation administrative agency has not thought about those aspects of the recreation experience outside the site it administers, and the typical highway department has not concerned itself with such matters.

In the remainder of this chapter we shall be concerned explicitly with the total recreation experience; and in other chapters we shall implicitly have it in mind, even when we speak only of the on-site aspects of the experience.

VISITS AND COSTS

The willingness and ability of ordinary people to enjoy outdoor recreation depends upon the costs of doing so. This general proposition can be made more precise and quantitative, at least on an illustrative basis.

We have noted that most outdoor recreation involves money costs and travel, and that all of it requires time for its enjoyment. "Costs" can therefore be expressed in dollars, in time, and in travel distance: all three are involved. For much outdoor recreation, these three measures will be highly correlated. That is, a long trip measured in miles is also likely to be a costly one, measured in dollars, and to require a relatively long time. Conversely, a trip for a short distance is likely to cost a lot less money and to take much less time.

If these three measures were invariably exactly in proportion, any one could be used as a measure for all three; and, since we usually think of costs in monetary terms, dollars would do to measure miles and time as well.

However, these measures of cost are not invariably correlated, and to some extent one kind of cost can substitute for another. One can think of situations where money costs are moderate but time costs large; a canoe trip may fall into this category. Or one may think of an expensive outdoor recreation experience that does not involve too much travel or time. Moreover, the kind of cost which will limit outdoor recreation activities will differ considerably, depending upon the circumstances of the individual. For the family whose money income is low, money costs are likely to be the most seriously limiting factor; for the man whose annual income is high, limitations of time are likely to be more restrictive. However, this man can stretch his time by using some of his money; he can, for instance, fly from his home city to an airport relatively near his vacation objective, and there rent a car, thus saving hours or days driving to and from. Likewise, the man with relatively high income may install air-conditioning or otherwise add to the comfort of his travel by car, assuming that he chooses to go that way.

We have spoken of costs as if they were obviously and uniquely observable and measurable. In fact, costs fall into different categories. The immediate cash costs of a particular recreation trip are one thing; the total costs, including replacement of equipment, may be much larger. When the family owns an auto capable of making the desired trip, and when it owns the various kinds of specialized equipment required, then cash costs may be low—limited to gasoline, food, and other direct expenditures. The family which begins camping must buy a considerable amount of equipment, thus making its first camping trip relatively far more expensive than later trips. But the time comes when all equipment must be replaced; the full costs of outdoor recreation must be met sooner or later, but not necessarily for each trip at the time. In planning its recreation activities, the family is perhaps influenced more by the immediate than by the long-run costs. However, in judging between two alternative sites or programs, it may well be that the ratio between direct costs is not much different than the ratio between total costs.

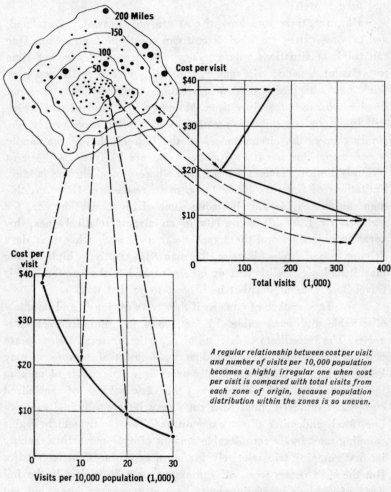

A regular relationship between cost per visit and number of visits per 10,000 population becomes a highly irregular one when cost per visit is compared with total visits from each zone of origin, because population distribution within the zones is so uneven.

Figure 9. Illustrating the effect of population distribution around a hypothetical recreation area, upon cost per visit, total visits, and visits per 10,000 population.

We can generalize this situation as follows: The number of recreation visits by one family to different areas or by different families to one area is inversely proportional to the costs incurred. As we shall note later, other factors, such as the family's preference for particular kinds of activities or for particular areas, may modify this relationship but not basically nullify it.

There is another set of factors which must be considered also. The desire to participate in outdoor recreation varies greatly among individuals. Some people go often, others go infrequently or not at all, even though income and other factors are comparable between the two. However, substantial numbers of people, if not selected for their interest in outdoor recreation, probably average out in terms of their basic interests. Thus, it is desirable to place the number of recreation visits on the basis of visits per 10,000 population in the particular area. For instance, we may have 1,000 visits to a particular state park for each 10,000 population in a particular city, and perhaps only 200 visits per 10,000 population from another city. We would expect a large city to have far more recreationists than a small one, all other factors equal; it is only by reducing visits to a per 10,000 base that these differences can be eliminated. This process is closely similar to the putting of food consumption on a per capita basis. A large country would obviously consume more food than a small one, but on a per capita basis they might consume the same.

A second generalization can be stated as follows: the total number of outdoor recreation visits from a particular city or other geographic area is directly proportional to the total population resident within it. As we shall note below, this generalization is affected by the first, and to some extent by other factors; but these do not nullify the validity of the generalization, in broad terms.

These general ideas can be illustrated with some data for a hypothetical artificial lake (Figure 9). The chief recreation activities at this lake are fishing, swimming, water sports generally, camping, and picnicking. Many people come from within 100 miles or so for all-day outings; and a few come from longer distances, staying overnight. It is thus typical of the intermediate type of area we described

47

in Chapter II. Those people who live within 50 miles of the lake are able to have a day at the lake for an average cost of $4 for a party of four. Partly as a result of this modest cost, 30,000 visits were recorded for the year, for each 10,000 persons in the total population—in other words, each person in this zone on the average visited the lake three times during the year. People who lived from 50 to 100 miles from the lake incurred higher costs—about $9 for a party of four, mostly for a single day but occasionally for an overnight visit; and probably as a result of this higher cost, the number of visits fell to 20,000 per 10,000 population. For the zones 100 to 150 miles and 150 to 200 miles, costs per party of four were $20 and $38, respectively; and visits per 10,000 of total population were 10,000 and 2,000, respectively. Thus, in general, there was a close inverse relation between cost per party visit and numbers of visitors per 10,000 total population. Our first generalization is rather closely borne out by these data.

But this is not the whole story. Total visits from each zone showed a somewhat different pattern, because total population in each zone differed. For instance, there were actually more visitors from the zone 50 to 100 miles away than there were from the closest zone, because total population was more than four times as great. There were many more visits in total from the 150 to 200 mile zone than from the 100 to 150 mile zone, because the former contained several relatively large cities, while the latter was entirely rural. Each distance zone takes in more total territory and usually more total population, and hence this tends to offset to some degree the decline in number of visits per 10,000 total population. The data on total numbers of visits thus in general supports our second generalization as to the effect of size of population in the tributary area for each recreation spot.

Other data from other areas support these findings. Visits to certain major national parks, to certain federal reservoirs, and to some metropolitan parks all show these twin characteristics of inverse relation to cost per visit and direct proportional relation to numbers of people in the tributary zone.

The foregoing is essentially a static type of analysis; it takes as given or fixed the numbers of people, their incomes, the travel facilities, the leisure patterns of the area's users, the existence of alternative recreation areas, the costs of visiting the latter (including entrance fees), and many other factors. As a matter of fact, some of these measures will change over time, and some means must be used of introducing their effect into these general relationships. This we propose to consider in the next section.

INCOME, TRANSPORTATION, AGE, AND OTHER FACTORS

We have noted that one of the four basic factors behind the sustained rise in use of outdoor recreation areas has been the increase in real income per capita. Not only have real incomes per capita risen, somewhat irregularly but still to a major degree over the years, but the proportions of income spent for recreation of all kinds and for outdoor recreation in particular have also risen. The available data on this point leave much to be desired. In the usual national income and expenditure data, "recreation" is defined to include only those items clearly and unequivocally used for recreation, such as movie admissions, purchase of golf clubs, and the like; no allowance is made for automobile and gasoline, food and shelter while travelling, and many other items purchased primarily for recreation— these latter are included under transportation, food, housing, clothing, and so on. Hence, the available data show direction of change in recreation expenditures better than they do absolute amounts.

The percentage of income spent for all recreation (as defined above) rose from about 3 per cent before the First World War to a peak of over 5 per cent by 1930; fell sharply during the severe depression years of the early 1930's and during the war years when many goods where unavailable to less than 4 per cent; after the war it rose again sharply, and in recent years has run somewhat over 5 per cent, with a mild tendency to increase further. Also according

49

to the above definition, the expenditures for outdoor recreation have increased from about 1/3 of 1 per cent before the war to nearly double that percentage today. As we have noted, the actual reported

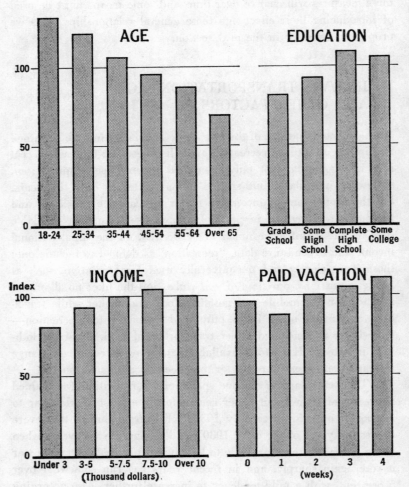

Figure 10. Net effect of various socio-economic factors on relative participation in all forms of outdoor recreation.

50

amount of these expenditures is relatively low because of the definition used, but the trend is perhaps significant. A steadily increasing percentage of a steadily rising real income per capita results in very large increases in actual sums spent for outdoor recreation. In 2000, with roughly double the present population, each with a real income roughly double today's average and with perhaps twice as large a percentage of that income spent for outdoor recreation, total expenditures for outdoor recreation might easily be eight times as large as at present.

At any given time, there is a considerable net relation between income per person or per family and the amount of outdoor recreation enjoyed (Figure 10). Families reporting $7,500 or more annual income had a third more total recreation activity than families reporting under $3,000 annual income, even when allowance is made for differences in education, leisure, and other factors. This was true even when many kinds of recreation, such as visiting with friends or relatives, which require little or no expenditure of cash, are included. The higher income families probably had more leisure, or at least more freedom from restrictive household and employment activities, and as a result probably had more energy left for outdoor recreation, as well as interest in it. The same general relationship, but more strikingly, holds for those kinds of outdoor recreation that require considerable expenditure for their enjoyment. Only a fourth of the families with incomes less than $3,000 took a vacation trip, while three-fourths of those with incomes of $10,000 and over did so. Similar relationships were found for other outdoor activities.

There is great variation among families in the amount of participation in outdoor recreation, regardless of the family income. That is, a small proportion of high income families will partake but little of outdoor recreation; and equally, a small proportion of low income families will have high participation in outdoor recreation. There is a general tendency, however, for participation in outdoor recreation and family income to be correlated. This is particularly marked at the lower income levels; as income rises, the effect of more income on total recreation activity is relatively less. In several studies, a tendency has been noted for the families of the very

51

highest incomes to have no more, and sometimes even less, outdoor recreation than families of only moderately high income. This suggests that time, taste, or other limitations are replacing the income restriction. However, the available data and experience are insufficient to be sure of this point.

A more marked effect of family income is upon the kind of outdoor recreation. Some kinds are usually much more expensive than others. Skiing and other winter sports, and canoeing and other boating, show participation rates four or five times as great in families of over $10,000 annual income as in families of under $3,000 income; in contrast, hunting, fishing, and hiking show a much more modest response to income. Moreover, there is good reason to believe that the luxury of a particular kind of outdoor recreation experience rises as people can afford it.

Transportation was also included as one of the four basic factors leading to greater outdoor recreation activity over the years. As we have noted, total travel has increased more than ten times in the past 50 years; while part of this has been in connection with everyday living, a major part is also for outdoor recreation. Nearly universal ownership of private autos and the development of good roads have been the two major factors concerned. But a significant proportion of the low income people still do not own autos, and their enjoyment of outdoor recreation is thereby greatly restricted. As a matter of fact, the development of private autos has been accompanied by—and has caused—a decline in public transportation facilities, so that the family without a private car is now often worse off than a few decades ago. The lack of a car is given as the major reason preventing outdoor recreation activity by about 5 per cent of all families; this is in addition to the more than half of all families reporting inadequate income for outdoor recreation.

The kind of road into an outdoor recreation area greatly affects its use. A few miles of dirt road effectively exclude the vast majority of outdoor users today—they either doubt their ability to negotiate the road or they prefer not to expose themselves to its discomforts. Paved roads designed for low speed travel or with inadequate capacity to accommodate all users also tend to limit or reduce recreation participation. Building major throughways often opens up relatively distant recreation areas to heavy usage by city or other people who formerly found the area too distant, in terms of time, for ready use.

As better transportation facilities are built, this has the effect of shifting the relationship between distance and cost, which we discussed earlier in this chapter. The actual money cost of a visit may be lowered; the time cost will almost certainly be less. As a result, the number of visits from a given distance zone will almost certainly rise. New curves to describe these relationships are thus required—the old curve, such as that presented in Figure 9, has shifted.

The amount and kind of outdoor recreation is also affected greatly by the age of the person concerned. Such activity rises rapidly as young people approach maturity; outdoor recreation is particularly the activity of the young adult, especially from eighteen to thirty-five years; and outdoor activities fall off steadily with advancing age. There is, of course, great variation among individuals in this respect. A few people over sixty-five have as heavy a participation rate as a few of the least active ones of eighteen. Some of the decline with age is due to the fact that certain kinds of outdoor recreation are more strenuous than some older people can stand, but the decline in activity also extends to the less strenuous activities, though less markedly so. Swimming is particularly an activity of the young: with 40 per cent of the people from eighteen to thirty-five going often, the proportion declines to less than 10 per cent for those over sixty-five. Approximately comparable declines are found for boating and canoeing, hunting, skiing and winter sports, and horseback riding. Fishing, on the other hand, holds up much better— older people partake of it about half as much as do young ones. And nature and bird walks actually show as much or more participation at older ages as at young ones.

These relationships of outdoor recreation and age are particularly important in view of the high probability of substantially more older people in the decades ahead. However, one must interpret these relationships with caution. The pattern of outdoor recreation activity by older people is heavily influenced by their personal experiences when young. Many of these older people perhaps never enjoyed outdoor recreation to the extent the young people of today do; and when the latter are old, they may engage in far more outdoor recreation than do the older people today. Moreover, it is highly probable that in the future the older people will enjoy much better health, have more strength, and have higher incomes than do old people today, thus lessening one of the factors leading to low participation today. However, it does seem probable that older people will always have somewhat different tastes and demands for outdoor recreation than will young ones.

There are also some differences in outdoor recreation activity between men and women. On the average, men engage in outdoor recreation somewhat more than do women, although there are great variations among each sex. Hunting is particularly a man's activity, fishing and boating less so. Hiking, bird and nature walks, picnicking, and camping are about equal between the sexes—the latter, at least, because they are usually family affairs in which all members of the family participate.

There are also some variations in outdoor recreation activity according to the education and occupation of the person concerned, although there are great differences among individuals in this respect. In general, outdoor recreation activity rises with educational attainment, at least up to some point; in part, this is because people of more education have more income, but there remains a significant net effect also. There is also some relation between outdoor recreation activity and occupation; the skilled worker and manager classes are highest, with laborers, service workers, and farmers the lowest (after differences in age and in income are removed from consideration).

Leisure was the fourth major factor affecting use of outdoor recreation which we considered in Chapter II. Unfortunately, we have little evidence as to the role of leisure today in explaining differences in recreation activities between individuals, except for differences in paid vacation. Only a fourth of those who have no paid vacation took a vacation trip, while two-thirds of those with four weeks or more paid vacation took trips; those with shorter paid vacations took vacation trips to an intermediate degree.

Such information as we have indicates that Negroes participate less in outdoor recreation that do whites. Several factors are probably responsible for this racial difference: Negroes frequently have lower incomes, they have often been excluded from certain outdoor recreation areas and hence are not as familiar with them, and their general cultural pattern sometimes seems to inhibit their participation in outdoor recreation. However, they are apparently coming in increasing numbers to participate in this activity.

This section on the characteristics of outdoor recreation users may perhaps be summarized briefly. The most significant fact is that people of all ages, both sexes, all income levels, all occupations, and of a wide variety of other characteristics, take part in outdoor recreation. In part, this widespread participation may be due to the fact that what we call outdoor recreation in fact consists of a wide variety of differing activities—something for each of the various groups mentioned. At the same time, there is undoubtedly a widespread, nearly universal appeal in the great outdoors and in the activities there. However, there are some differences in the degree of participation in outdoor recreation. Young adults, those of moderately high income, those of above average education, those in skilled occupations and managerial jobs, and those of the white race, participate more than do their opposites. Very poor people, those in bad health or infirm, the very young and the very old, of the lowest occupational levels, participate far less. It is probable, although we lack specific information, that these differences are greatest for the distant resource-based outdoor recreation areas, and are perhaps least for the nearby user-oriented areas.

EFFECT OF
SPATIAL DISTRIBUTION OF POPULATION

In an earlier section of this chapter, we showed how the number of visitors to a recreation area is related to distance from their home to the spot, and also to the number of people in the zone of origin. A few more comments on the latter point are appropriate, because the spatial distribution of population greatly affects the total use or demand for recreation at a particular recreation spot.

How this works may be illustrated with a hypothetical case. Imagine two outdoor recreation areas, approximately the same in all relevant features; imagine further that the populations in the tributary areas are also closely similar as to total numbers (but not spatial distribution), income, age distribution, education, occupation, and any other characteristics that might affect their outdoor recreation activity; and assume further that patterns of leisure and transportation are closely similar. One might then jump to the conclusion that the number of visitors to each area would be the same, or nearly so; but this may be far from the case. For one recreation area, the bulk of the population—the major city or cities of the tributary region—might lie quite close to the recreation area—or, perhaps more accurately, we might say that the recreation area lies quite close to the major city or cities. In this case, the proportion of the total potential users who could visit the recreation area at relatively low cost would be high, and they would presumably come in relatively large numbers. For the other recreation area, the major source of visitors, from a large city or cities, might lie at considerable distance. For these people, the cost (in money, time, and travel) of visiting the recreation area would be relatively large, and consequently few people would visit it, although the basic demand curve for the two populations was the same.

This matter is far from academic. Visits to certain national parks illustrate this idea well. Visits are very heavy to Yosemite and to Great Smoky national parks, for instance, largely because each is relatively close to large populations. California people use Yosemite very heavily on week ends, in a manner somewhat similar to the way some state parks are used; if it lay another 300 miles farther away from the San Francisco Bay and Los Angeles regions, its use in this way would be very much less than at present. In contrast, Grand Canyon National Park has a relatively very much smaller total population within the same distance, and hence most of its visitors come from much farther away; thus total visits to Grand Canyon are less than they otherwise would be. The comparison is even more striking if one takes Mount McKinley National Park in Alaska, or Isle Royale National Park in Lake Superior, or some of the more remote national monuments; for these, most of the potential visitors live at long distances away, and use is very light as a consequence. Other factors, such as the inherent attractiveness of the various areas, operate also, of course, but spatial distribution of population is one major factor.

The same relationships hold for state parks or private recreation areas. A major factor affecting their potential use or patronage is their location with respect to major centers of population. Attractive mountain and lake areas in southern New England, New York State, Pennsylvania, and adjacent areas are relatively close to the largest population centers of the nation; similar areas in the Ozarks have a much smaller potential clientele within the same distances. Within these general regions, major differences in spatial distribution of population also exist.

EFFECT OF ALTERNATIVE AREAS

Another major factor affecting the recreation use of any particular area is the number, characteristics, and variety of alternative areas available to the population in the tributary zones (Figure 11). Frequently, the relationship of the various areas is competitive; that is, use of one tends to diminish use of other similar areas, perhaps not to exactly the same degree. Sometimes, however, the different areas

57

may be complementary or supplementary, in the sense that the availability of one tends actually to increase use of the other. For instance, it might be that few people would care to acquire boats and motors merely to use one medium-size artificial lake; but if several such lakes were available, they might find it worth while to acquire boats, with the result that use of each lake tended to increase use of the other. In still other cases, two areas or kinds of areas might be

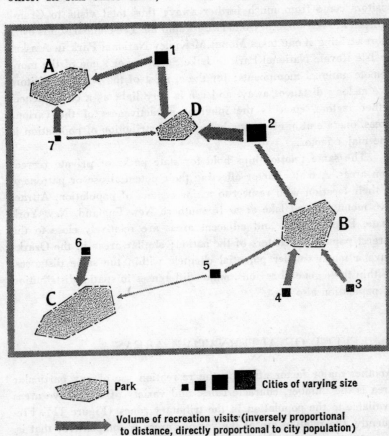

Figure 11. Hypothetical relations of cities of various sizes with sample rural parks.

independent, in the sense that use of each had no effect upon the other; mountain areas might neither compete with nor supplement seashore areas, for instance. While we can readily imagine many relationships, as a matter of fact this aspect of outdoor recreation has been studied relatively little.

In western Nebraska, use of each of three artificial lakes, primarily for fishing, depended largely upon their location relative to the other lakes. For these lakes, almost no one was willing to travel more than 60 to 80 miles (one way) for a day's outing. If there was no alternative lake within this distance, the number of visits was inversely and rather clearly proportional to the distance from the user's home to the lake, and hence to the cost of a visit. If there was an alternative lake within this distance, people tended to divide their patronage between the two lakes, some going to one and some to the other, or the same people sometimes going to one and sometimes to the other. However, interestingly enough, total visits to two (or three lakes, if the third were also close) tended to be higher than to one alone; that is, people not merely divided their total recreational use, but they also tended to make somewhat more total use than if only one lake had existed.

A generalization may be offered at this point: a major factor influencing the use of any recreation area is the existence and location of other recreation areas. The nature of this relationship may vary, and the effect may be strong or weak; but it is impossible to consider one area alone, and expect to arrive at accurate estimates of recreation usage.

The relationship discussed for western Nebraska existed even though no entrance fee was charged for any lake. If, however, use of one recreation area was permitted only by payment of a fee, while use of alternative areas was free, this would surely affect the division of use between them. The effect of differences in fees in shifting use from one lake to another would be small if the fees were small, if the areas had other outstanding characteristics, and if other costs of visiting them were in any case high; and, conversely, the effect of entrance fees in shifting use from one area to another

would be large if the difference in fees were great, if the areas themselves did not differ significantly in their attractiveness, or if other
costs of visiting each were relatively low.

This matter of the effect of entrance fees on relative use of outdoor recreation areas may find great significance as between publicly and privately provided areas. Entrance fees to public areas
have traditionally been low or even absent. Within the past few
years, some state park systems have introduced a system of wind-
shield stickers; a sticker must be purchased if the user is to stay
overnight in the park, for instance. But, since such stickers are
customarily good for the entire season, any use beyond the first one
is still without extra charge—"free," as it were. As long as equally
attractive public areas are available free, it is very difficult to build
up much patronage for privately provided areas on a fee basis. The
private areas, under these circumstances, will be used only to the
extent they are more attractive or less crowded. One should not leap
to the conclusion that all that is needed for financial success of the
private areas is the imposition of a fee on the public areas; it may
well be that the potential use of the private areas is too small, or
the necessary costs of management and operation too large, or both,
for the private area to be financially successful no matter what
charges were imposed for the public area.

But fees might well affect use of different units of a publicly
provided outdoor recreation system also. If fees are imposed on some
areas but not on others of similar character and location, this will
tend to shift use toward the no-fee or low-fee areas and away from
the high-fee areas; the effect would obviously be greater, the greater
the difference in fees and the larger this sum in comparison with
other costs of visiting the areas. This substitution effect should be
considered in establishing any system of fees for public areas. One
might wish to avoid changing the pattern of use of different areas,
in which case fees should be similar or proportional in the different
areas. Or he might wish to use fees as an instrument in effecting
changes in use pattern, either from one area to another or from one
time of use to another. For instance, entrance fees might be imposed

for week-end use but not for weekday use; again, the effectiveness of this device would depend upon the level of the fees charged and upon their relation to other costs of visiting the areas in question. It should be added that the device of different charges ("discriminatory pricing," in the economist's jargon) is widely used in private business; movie admissions, golf, and many other activities are cheaper at one hour of the day or one day of the week than at other hours or days. Deliberate variations in user fees as a management tool have been used hardly at all in management of public recreation areas, yet there seem great possibilities in this direction. It should be further pointed out that this provides the potential user with a wide field for individual choice; he can go at the most popular time at a relatively high fee, or he can go at other times at a lower fee or free. From the viewpoint of the agency, it is a way of making the same physical facilities serve a wider range of demand than would otherwise be the case.

POLICY ISSUES

The information presented in this chapter leads to a consideration of some policy issues. First of all, for which parts of the total public should outdoor recreation be provided by public or governmental action? One is tempted to say at once: for all sectors of the general public. Surely, people of all ages, incomes, classes, races, occupations, etc., use outdoor recreation, if given the opportunity, as we have noted; why should not public recreation areas be available for all of them, and not merely for some? But, as we have noted, in practice some sectors of the total population use outdoor recreation far more than do others; or, possibly more accurately, some sectors use it far less than do others. In particular, lower income classes use it very little, simply because they cannot afford it. It is all very well to say that the national park system, for instance, is open to everyone, without discrimination; but, in fact, it is as effectively closed to the poorest one-third or one-tenth of the total population as if "no entrance" signs had been posted for these people. State parks, which can be visited more cheaply, are still practically unavailable to a significant segment of the total population. Even city parks, with no entrance fees and no cash costs of getting from home to park, may be unavailable to many people, simply because they are located where use is impossible or because they are so crowded. One might argue that public parks *should*, as a matter of policy, be provided only for those classes which pay for them through their income, property, or other taxes. Many people who would reject this argument on philosophic or ideological grounds may yet not realize that in practice this is what many public outdoor recreation programs do. If we have convictions on policy, we should be determined to carry them out in terms of actual programs.

This general issue may be narrowed down a little: how can the needs of the poorer people for outdoor recreation be met most effectively? Shall government at some level (usually the city) provide at least some outdoor recreation facilities for everyone, no matter how crowded the area and how costly the land? Is there a public obligation to provide a more extensive type of outdoor recreation for the poor people of city centers (and slums), outside of the city or at least on the outskirts of it? If it is necessary to provide them free transportation to such areas, is this part of the public obligation, also? What about free or highly subsidized trips for some segments of the total population—school children, for instance—to still more distant areas or for longer experiences, such as camping? How, if at all, may we bring some taste of the national parks to those people who can never hope to visit one in person? What about colored films and sound movies?

Still another range of policy questions turns on the degree to which we wish consciously to use outdoor recreation as a democratizing force in the nation. Schools, churches, housing and many other facets of modern urban life in the United States tend to be socially structured—racially structured, but also income and class structured. Because of its nearly universal appeal, outdoor recreation might well be a major democratizing force; outdoor sports have operated in this direction, often without specific intent to do so. Many people in the recreation field would oppose conscious use of outdoor recreation for this purpose, yet others would support it. Certainly, since it has possibilities, it does pose policy problems.

How far should entrance or user fees be used as a recreation management tool? This is very closely related to the matter of using entrance fees as a means of paying for public outdoor recreation areas, a subject to which we return in more detail in Chapter VII. If one rejects entrance fees under any and all circumstances, then of course they are not available as a park or recreation area management tool. But some people might reluctantly accept entrance fees because this is the only way they could obtain desired recreation areas, but would insist on uniform charges to all persons at all times. They might defend this as fair and equitable. Others might defend fees at times when the parks were crowded and no fees at other times, as a way of spreading use more evenly. Certainly, this is a matter with many ramifications that should be considered carefully before a final judgment is reached.

63

4

LAND AND WATER RESOURCES
USED FOR
OUTDOOR RECREATION

OUTDOOR RECREATION, BY ITS VERY NATURE, RE-
quires land and water resources—sometimes, considerable areas of
land and volumes of water. The purpose of this chapter is to present
some of the basic facts on the areas and volumes involved now and
likely to be required in the future, and some of the resource utiliza-
tion problems thus arising.

ROLE OF PRIVATELY OWNED AREAS

Although our primary concern in this book is with publicly owned
outdoor recreation areas, we may start with a brief consideration of
the use of privately owned areas for recreation. As noted previously,

little direct information is available on this subject. Some people own land and water areas for their own use and enjoyment; these may be either solely for recreation, as a cottage at the seashore or in the mountains, or they may nominally be for other purposes, as a ranch or forest where the recreation value to the owner is a major consideration. Some land and water is owned by one individual but is used by others for recreation, on payment of a fee. Camping areas are thus provided in some circumstances. Or permission to hunt upon private land may be sold by the owner of the land to other persons; the game itself belongs to the state, and cannot be sold, but permission to enter private land for hunting can be sold. Some large land-owning companies—forest industry corporations and public utility companies, in particular—allow the general public to engage in outdoor recreation on their land, often free of charge, and sometimes provide facilities for the comfort of the users. In these latter cases, recreation is usually not the only, or even primary, kind of land use, but is subordinate to other major land uses, such as forestry.

It is unfortunate that we have so little information about public use of private land and water for recreation. With the large increase in demand for outdoor recreation which is imminent, more and more interest will arise for public use of such areas. A number of important policy issues arise, to which we shall return later in this chapter. More accurate and detailed information about present use of such areas would help to provide answers to these questions.

CITY PARKS

The prime example of the user-oriented type of outdoor recreation area is the city park. A few such parks are located outside the city's legal boundaries, in some instances some miles away; but, typically, city parks are located close to where city people live. Moreover, they are the chief, often the only kind, of public outdoor recreation area available to most city people. To a substantial degree, therefore, city

65

parks are synonymous with user-oriented outdoor recreation. Information about them is rather limited. The National Recreation Association, a private organization, has conducted censuses at periodic intervals—five-year intervals at present, although more frequently at an earlier time. Response to requests for information is voluntary, and hence incomplete to an unknown degree. Some information is available from Bureau of Census inquiries to cities, but this relates primarily to expenditures.

A distinguishing characteristic of the city park is its emphasis upon use and activity, rather than upon area. That is, a minimum area, of minimum suitable characteristics, is essential; but primary emphasis is put upon the use and activity on the available areas, not upon their extent or physical characteristics. In these ways, city parks differ greatly from the resource-based outdoor recreation areas, where primary consideration is given to area, and secondary consideration to activity. However, our data upon use of these areas is particularly deficient, primarily because their use is generally so informal and easy, with no attendance records taken.

In 1955, there were over 20,000 city parks in the United States, with about ¾ million acres of land. The average city park thus had about 37 acres. Like many averages, this included much variation. In the New York metropolitan region, playground areas averaged four acres each, playfields eleven acres, small parks five acres, and large local parks nearly 57 acres, for instance. A city park may be little more than a small square, with perhaps a statue and a few benches; or it may contain several hundred acres, in exceptional cases such as Central Park in New York or Rock Creek Park in Washington, with many diverse activities possible; or it may be at any intermediate situation. Each type has its particular purposes and uses, and together a wide variety of sizes and kinds of areas make up a well-rounded city park system.

A commonly used standard for city parks is ten acres per 1,000 people within the city, and an additional ten acres of larger "regional" parks outside the city or in other special locations. A broad standard such as this cannot be applied everywhere; as we noted in Chapter II, park acreage to this standard would require more land

66

than is available on Manhattan Island. For the New York metropolitan region, only about a fifth of the total population lived where the standard of ten acres was even approximately met; more than 60 per cent of the people lived where fewer than four acres per 1,000 population were available. This standard must be considered more as a goal than as an actuality. If even the minimal standard of ten acres had been applied to all cities, then 2 million acres of city park land would have been required in 1955, rather than the 3/4 million acres actually available. With the probable increases in urban population in prospect, by 2000 as much as 5 million acres of city parks would be required to meet this standard. It is most improbable that any such area can be provided. In the older cities, where present areas are deficient, it is difficult to add new park area, although sometimes this is done on a small scale with urban renewal projects. In the new suburbs, it is difficult to get land reserved for park purposes before it gets built on.

It is most unfortunate that we lack any reliable estimate of the value of land in city parks. It is altogether possible that the value of the raw land, without improvement, in all city parks is as great as the similar value of all state parks or of all federal areas devoted primarily to recreation, in spite of the vastly greater area of the latter. The value of improvements on city park land is not large, compared to the value of the land itself. Many people mistakenly assume that the land has a low value because it does not have expensive structures on it.

STATE PARKS

State parks are one of the two best examples of publicly owned intermediate outdoor recreation areas. (Federal reservoirs, which we take up next, are the other.) A few state parks are of the resource-based type, with unusual natural features broadly comparable to those in national parks and national forests; a few are very similar to some city parks, in that they are relatively small and close to large urban centers, to provide similar types of recreation. On the whole, however, the state parks conform to our definition of intermediate areas. They mostly lie some miles from the bulk of users, but not so far but what day-long use is their chief use.

In 1955, there were about 5 million acres in all state parks. However, 2.2 million acres of this were in the Adirondack Forest Reserve of New York State, and another 1 million acres in seven other large parks of over 50,000 acres each, two of which were also in New York, two in California, and one each in Maine, Michigan, and South Dakota. The more than 2,000 remaining state parks thus had about 1.9 million acres, or less than 1,000 acres each; one-third of these had less than 50 acres each. Many of the latter included a small lake with swimming beach, a small picnic area, and little more. Great diversity in size and type of area thus characterizes the state park system.

Park specialists have not established standards for adequacy in area of state park systems, comparable to the standards for city parks. Some states have adopted goals for park adequacy, but measured on a distance or time basis. These goals differ widely from state to state. A state park within 25 miles, or within two hours' driving time, or within some other time or distance standard, for all or for most of their people are goals in some states. However, these have not been translated into acreage standards. On the basis of the experience in some of the states with good, but not the most outstanding, state park systems, it would appear that 30 acres of state park land for each 1,000 state population is a reasonable present-day standard. Some states far exceed this now. If the states with lesser area were brought up to this standard, about 10 million acres of state parks would be required today. With the probable future growth in recreation demand, an adequate area in 2000 would require 50 million acres of state park land. This assumes average use per acre would about double, compared with present use.

State parks will play a major role in the outdoor recreation picture of the future. For one thing, their area can be expanded more readily than can that of either city or national parks. The adjustments possible in location mean that state parks are less demanding than city parks; the adjustments possible in quality of resources mean they are less demanding than are national parks. Within the limits of location and of resource characteristics, thousands of sites and millions of acres are potential state parks. Some investment and considerable management are required to turn potential sites into actual park areas, but there are still greater possibilities here than for either of the other two major kinds of outdoor recreation areas.

City parks are exclusively for outdoor recreation, broadly defined; state parks are almost equally so. Other state areas, such as forests, may have a considerable recreation potential, although primarily for other purposes.

USE OF FEDERAL RESERVOIRS
FOR RECREATION

Although the federal government has been building reservoirs and other water control works for a long time, its activity in this field has been greatest in the past 30 years. Reservoirs are built to hold major flood flows, and thus reduce the hazard of floods—but not to give complete flood "protection," in spite of much misunderstanding to the contrary. They are also built to provide irrigation water supplies, and to provide storage for hydroelectric power generation. More commonly, a reservoir provides more than one of these services. Almost no large reservoirs have been created primarily or solely for recreation, but most of the reservoirs built for other purposes have significant recreation potentials. In some cases, the dam and associated works is itself a prime attraction for tourists and other recreationists. The water body also has major usefulness for various water sports, in many cases. Small reservoirs primarily for outdoor recreation have been built in some state parks.

In 1960, 250 reservoirs built by the Corps of Engineers, containing 5.3 million acres in total and 3.9 million acres in the recreation pool acreage, were open for recreation; and in that year these reservoirs had 106 million visits. In that same year, 29 reservoirs operated by TVA, with over 1 million acres, were also available for recreation. By 1960 the Bureau of Reclamation had built 178 reservoirs with an area of 2 million acres, also open to recreation; most of these are actually administered, as far as outdoor recreation is concerned, by other federal, state, and local agencies. As noted above, none of these reservoirs was built primarily or solely for outdoor recreation; yet, on many of them, recreation is certainly now a major use.

The rate of growth in recreation use of these reservoirs has been especially rapid, when compared with the growth in outdoor recreation in general. Many of these reservoirs have been located in parts of the United States lacking in natural water bodies. A large proportion are in the Great Plains, for instance. In these regions, water sports were obviously impossible until water bodies were available. The combination of new water bodies and the general postwar boom in water sports has led to an extremely rapid rise in water recreation in these regions.

Since these reservoirs were constructed primarily for other uses, their recreation use is, in a sense, a windfall to the outdoor recreation field. Some of them are well located with respect to population centers; others are more remote and hence less used. It is not realistic to talk about an adequate area of such reservoirs, for recreation is not the purpose for which they were built. Likewise, it is not possible to say how many such reservoirs or how large an area should be planned for the future for outdoor recreation. It is fairly certain that many more such reservoirs will be built in the future, for the same primary purposes as underlay those built in the past, and that these additional reservoirs will have large outdoor recreation values. As much as 20 million acres of reservoir and surrounding area available for recreation may come into use by 2000.

WATER FOR RECREATION

A great deal of outdoor recreation requires or uses water. However, this use does not "consume" water in the same sense that irrigation consumes water. Recreation is dependent upon a body of water or upon a flowing stream of water. Data do not permit us to say what proportion of all water surfaces, natural or artificial, is used for outdoor recreation, or to what degree; and the same is true of streams and other moving water. However, it seems probable that a substantial proportion of all such water bodies is used for recreation to some degree. As we have noted previously, the variety of water uses for recreation is very great, and the requirements for the various uses differ considerably. While many areas are used very intensively—too much so, in some cases, for their greatest enjoyment—it is also true that many other areas are used much less intensively than is physically possible. Lack of easy access, or considerable distance from where users live, or lack of facilities such as launching ramps, and other factors are responsible for light usage in many instances.

As total recreation demand in the future mounts, so will the demand upon water for this purpose. It is not possible to put this demand in terms of acre feet or cubic feet per second, or of any other measure of volume or flow, for the reason, mentioned above, that recreation does not consume water in this sense. Recreation usage of a reservoir may create management problems; for example, drawdowns for other purposes may impair the value of the reservoir for recreation. It is conceivable that all recreation demands for water could be met without depriving any city, industry, or farm of any water required by it. The biggest future problem in provision of water for outdoor recreation is not volume, but quality. One consequence of our growing population, increasing urbanization, and mounting industrial output is the vastly increased volume of pollution which is typically dumped into the most convenient water body. If water is to be used for recreation, it must be relatively clean; this is true whether the use is for swimming, boating, fishing, or most any other use. Recreation and pollution disposal are likely to come into direct conflict, as future water uses. In each case, aesthetics is perhaps more important than economics. How dirty water will we play in or on?

FEDERAL LAND FOR RECREATION

As we noted in Chapter II, the federal government owns one-third of the land surface of the United States, in the proprietary as well as in the jurisdictional sense, if Alaska is included, and one-fifth if it is omitted. By far the greater part of this area is used primarily for forestry, grazing, or other uses, but has important recreational values; some is used primarily for recreation.

From the viewpoint of recreation, the most important federal areas are parts of the national park system. In 1960, this system included 29 national parks, 83 national monuments, and 74 other areas of various designations, with a total area of over 25 million acres. Units of this system are supposed to be unique in some sense, with national significance; some are scenic, others historical, scientific, or for other reasons unique. In 1961, total visits to the national park system were 79 million. A system of 343 federal wildlife refuges, containing 28 million acres, has as its main objective the protection of important and endangered species of wildlife, including waterfowl. In the broadest sense, these are recreational areas also; the objective of protecting the wildlife is recreational, not economic in the narrower sense. These areas also provided direct recreational experience; in 1960, they had 11 million visits.

There are 155 national forests, containing 182 million acres. These are multiple-use lands, for the most part, and recreation is recognized as an important use. On 15 million acres of wilderness and on a comparatively small area of campgrounds and other specialized recreation areas, recreation is the primary or sole use. In 1960, the national forests had 92 million visits. Under the supervision of the Bureau of Land Management is a large area of federal land, known by various terms (public domain, grazing districts, Oregon and California revested lands, etc.), which for the most part is managed under a program of multiple-use administration generally similar to that on the national forests. In general, these lands do not have the recreation potential of the national forests, yet they are increasingly used for this purpose.

72

These various kinds of federal land are prime examples of resource-based public outdoor recreation areas. The national parks and part of the national forests are the finest areas the nation has to offer, and many are world famous. Others are less outstanding but still unusually good. While some people live near these areas, most people live considerable distances away, requiring relatively long travel to reach them. For this reason, most visits to these areas are vacation travel.

It is almost impossible to set a standard of "adequacy" for resource-based outdoor recreation areas. If standards for eligibility are kept high, relatively few areas can meet them. It can well be argued that any and all areas meeting the very high standards should be set aside for this purpose. The difficulty is that the standards are subjective—dependent upon the viewpoints and personal values of the person appraising them. There can be little disagreement today that Grand Canyon, Yellowstone, and other famous national parks are unique. There may be more doubt about some of the lesser-known areas or about some of the proposed additions to the park system. Some of the national forest areas are equally fine, and it can be argued that they should be transferred to park status; the only significant difference would probably be that, as national parks, they would be closed to mining, lumbering, and grazing, to which they are open as forests. But in some cases this would not be significant because their value for these purposes would be low in any case.

It is still harder to suggest a desirable future level of "adequacy" for the areas of this kind. Some areas not now in federal ownership may be added. Several seashore areas have been proposed, as have areas along the shores of the Great Lakes; a prairie national park has been suggested; and various free-flowing natural rivers are prime candidates for some form of public ownership and control. In considering additions to the area of resource-based federal recreation areas, one should carefully distinguish them from two other kinds of additions to federal areas. Proposals have been made for substantial additions of areas of an essentially intermediate type, to provide outdoor recreation for large numbers of people, where needed, but without the special qualities of the resource-based areas. Other pro-

73

posals have been made to transfer some areas from national forest to national park status; while important in some respects, this is not a net addition to federal ownership. There simply are not in existence today large areas of high quality resource-based outdoor recreation sites which are not now in public ownership. Even if all the areas proposed for inclusion were to be added, their net addition to area would be small relative to present areas, although significant in absolute acreage.

CAPACITY OF RECREATION RESERVES IN RELATION TO THEIR AREA

Although all outdoor recreation requires relatively large areas of land and water for its enjoyment, the intensity of land use varies greatly between one kind of outdoor recreation and another, and between one area and another of the same general kind. For all the resource-based publicly owned outdoor recreation areas as a group, use now runs in the general magnitude of one visit per acre annually; for the publicly owned intermediate type of areas as a group, use is about 40 visits per acre annually; and for the public user-oriented areas as a group, use averages over 1,500 visits per acre annually. There are great differences between areas in each group, some of the more heavily used of the resource-based running as high as or higher than the lower units of the intermediate, and similarly between the latter and the user-oriented. Moreover, there are great differences in intensity of use within many units of each. The more heavily used, more popular spots within the resource-based and intermediate areas probably have use intensities as high as or higher than average intensities for the whole user-oriented group; and within the latter some units must have use intensities several times the average. Conversely, of course, each type of area has some spots where use is very low.

The intensity of recreation use has surely increased in the past, especially so on the resource-based areas, probably less so on the intermediate areas, and probably least of all on the user-oriented areas. While total use has increased on all types, and at rates not too

74

greatly divergent, the area changes for the various types have been inverse to these probable changes in intensity. With the probable rise in total recreation activity in the future, intensity of use will almost certainly rise much further. While major increases in acreage are possible and, in the author's opinion desirable, it seems unlikely that they can be large enough to offset the expected increases in total use. The probability of further increases in intensity of use, when in the opinion of many observers many areas are already overcrowded, raises some major problems.

What constitutes proper intensity of use of a recreation area? Or, stated differently, what constitutes overcrowding? The answer depends in part upon the physical nature of the area in question, in part upon the kinds of activities carried on, and mostly upon our own attitudes. In a wilderness area, if the basic quality of the wilderness experience is to be maintained, one cannot encounter many other recreationists—perhaps only one or two other parties each day. If more people than this are encountered, the character of the area and of the experience changes; it becomes essentially an extensive outdoor recreation area, with a relatively natural environment but with active public use. The interference of one group with another is rarely physical, under these circumstances, but is psychological. Use at this standard means perhaps no more than 600 person-days of outdoor recreation annually per million acres, the exact figure depending to some extent on the degree to which topography tends to concentrate the few visitors along natural routes and trails.

At the other extreme, one boy on a playing field is lost; he can enjoy the area for its prime purpose only when several of his fellows are also there. But too many boys on one playing field can overcrowd it, too, making its prime activity less satisfying. Within these extremes, many intermediate possibilities exist. Recreation specialists can establish broad ranges of suitable use intensity, for different kinds of areas. Some of these have solid physical bases; too many people trying to swim in one body of water means so much direct physical interference as to render the whole activity impractical, for instance. In many cases, however, the limits are based upon our ideas of suitable degrees of privacy and companionship. A common rule in the Forest Service is three campgrounds per acre, for instance; one can crowd several times this number of tents and other camp equipment onto an acre, if absolutely necessary, but the result would be a severe reduction in privacy. On the other hand, most campers prefer to camp where others are in sight, rather than to be completely alone. While recreation specialists have certain standards or general rules, these are far from invariable from agency to agency or from state to state, and in almost no case do they rest upon solid research and empirical study.

While it is possible to estimate capacity of outdoor recreation areas for various kinds of activity, yet considerable flexibility in rates of use is possible. Moreover, the intensity of use can often be increased, without too severe loss in quality, by means of capital investment. A grassed playing field can sustain only a certain level of use, for instance; but the same area, when black-topped, may sustain use at several times that rate. Skillful plantings of appropriate shrubs can often provide a measure of privacy in a camp or picnic area, for example. In the most intensively used downtown parks and play areas, each foot of land may be used intensively, and two- or more-storey outdoor recreation areas may well be necessary in the future. By roads and paths, the more remote parts of larger areas can often be opened up for use, thus reducing the load on the most popular spots.

In the end, however, there is some absolute limit to intensity of recreation use of an area, if it is to maintain its original purpose. In this respect, recreation capacity for an area is roughly comparable to grazing capacity for range areas or to sustained yield capacity for forest areas. Natural conditions of climate, soil, and other factors limit output from these other areas; fertilizer, irrigation, and many intensive cultural practices can step up their output, though often at excessive cost. Because psychological rather than physical, the limits to intensity of recreation areas are less easily measured and probably less rigid; yet they exist, and it is unwise to disregard them. A national park could be converted into an intensive urban park, for instance, with usage several times as great as at present, but it would no longer be a national park.

One major factor in this matter of intensity of use is the time distribution of such use as does occur. Typically, outdoor recreation areas experience extremely uneven use. A city park may be crowded at some hours of the day, nearly empty at others; state parks typically get much heavier use on week ends than during the week; and resource-based areas are often not used at all during off-seasons. The time pattern of use is extreme, compared to most time patterns of human activity. This presents a major management problem. If enough capacity is provided for the peak demand, then most of the capacity is idle nearly all of the time. Total costs for an area and for its improvements are often closely correlated with peak capacity, rather than with average use. Thus, to provide capacity for the peak demand means relatively high costs, in relation to the use actually made over a longer period. On the other hand, if some degree of overuse is permitted at peak periods, costs can be lower, but other disadvantages arise. The Forest Service, for instance, often provides enough campground capacity to care for demand on a normal summer week end, allowing some degree of overcrowding on July 4 and on Labor Day. No one likes to plan for overuse, yet this may be the least unsatisfactory management method where demand is so extremely uneven between one time period and another. One objective of recreation management may be to shift some of the use from periods of excessive demand to periods of demand less than capacity. One means of doing this can be by fees or charges during periods of excess demand and no fees, or lower ones, during periods of lower demand. We shall return to this subject in Chapter VII.

COMPETING DEMANDS FOR LAND AND WATER

All, or nearly all, natural resources in the United States are in demand for some use now; and with the prospective increases in total population and national income, demands for resources in general will rise. However, the natural resource situation for the United States is not tight, let alone acute; our future economic

77

growth and welfare will not be seriously restricted, if at all, by resource scarcity. Future demands on all kinds of natural resources will be manageable, although some problems will exist. The use of land and water resources for outdoor recreation must be evaluated in light of the general natural resource situation.

In agriculture, crop surpluses have existed for several years, and the consensus of informed experts in the field is that surpluses will continue to come into being during the next few decades, if not longer. The need for cropland will become less, at least in the next two decades, rather than more. The rapid and major technological advances in agriculture are the reason underlying this situation of relative surplus. In forestry, the demand for lumber, plywood, paper, and other forest products will be high, at least at present prices for these products, and possibly beyond the capacity of our forests to meet. Yet it seems improbable that there will be a major increase in commercial forest area; for one thing, the costs of converting relatively small parcels of nonforest land into large productive forests is probably too great, especially considering the length of time required, for it to be economic. The demand for water will rise, especially for urban, industrial, and pollution disposal uses. Yet enough water exists, if we are willing to pay the necessary costs of getting and purifying it.

Physically, ample resources for outdoor recreation exist. The problem is primarily one of the necessary costs of making such resources available for this purpose, and of improving and managing them. Enough resources to provide a satisfactory area for outdoor recreation can be spared from other uses, without serious impingement upon the latter. But the nation, and its various localities, must face the issue of the amounts it is prepared to spend for recreation.

QUALITY OF
OUTDOOR RECREATION EXPERIENCE

Reference has been made in various places to the effects of crowding and of improper use upon the quality of the recreation experience.

78

It seems worth while to consider the matter briefly but more explicitly. It is easy today to see the rising demand for outdoor recreation, if one considers only the numbers of visits to various kinds of areas. But, to what extent does the rising volume of use mean only a lowering in quality of experience? Is overcrowding occurring; does this mean a less desirable experience; and are more people simply dividing the same or less total recreational value?

These are not simple questions to answer, even if one is able and willing to face the facts objectively. The quality of a recreation experience is not easily measured. What deeply stirs one person may leave another cold. One may unthinkingly or deliberately trample under foot a rare plant, while another may treasure and admire it intensely. One may be deeply impressed by a geyser pool, while another regards it as an interesting place to throw an empty beer can. Social scientists have long agreed that it is extremely difficult to compare the emotional or psychological satisfactions and pains of one individual with those of another.

Yet differences in quality of outdoor recreation experience do exist, and we would be seriously remiss if we were to ignore them. Some kinds of outdoor recreation experience are typically more meaningful than others: a visit to a national shrine, such as the Lincoln Memorial in Washington or Independence Hall in Philadelphia, or to such an awesome natural wonder as Grand Canyon or Old Faithful, is a far deeper experience for most people than a simple picnic in a park or an informal game on a playing field. But there are also differences in the quality of response of one person compared with another for the same experience. The teenager who knows something of his country's history will be far more impressed by and interested in Independence Hall or Jamestown than one who has been indifferent to such history. Likewise, the visitor to a wilderness area or relatively undisturbed national park or forest, who knows something of the ecology of the environment, will gain far more from it than one who merely sees it as "pretty" scenery.

The quality of the outdoor recreation experience can be maintained or improved in several ways. First of all, the area itself should be suitably maintained in the physical sense; almost no one enjoys a littered and dirty area as much as a clean one. The area can often be laid out so that people can see but not injure. Above all, programs of education, at the site and elsewhere, can help people to know what they see, what it means, and thus to enjoy it more. Children and adults who engage in outdoor sports invariably enjoy them more when they do them moderately well than if they do them poorly. The standard for outdoor recreation areas should not be, how many people came through here, but, rather, how much difference did it make to those who came.

SUBSTITUTION IN OUTDOOR RECREATION

The requirements and demands for outdoor recreation are not absolute, but are relative to many other factors. The desire for certain kinds of outdoor recreation may exist in an individual or in a group, but its fulfillment depends upon opportunity. Moreover, even the desire itself may depend upon past opportunity. There is relatively little desire for swimming among a population which has never experienced it, for instance. But even people who want very much to swim will probably engage in some other activity if no opportunity exists for swimming. They may substitute some other outdoor recreation activity for swimming, or they may substitute some other kind of activity for outdoor recreation.

This substitutability provides a desirable degree of flexibility in provision and management of outdoor recreation areas. If demands were inflexible and unvarying, it would often be very costly to provide certain kinds of opportunity in environments not conducive to them. Water sports would be very costly in desert areas, for instance. Moreover, the possibility of substitution means that it is unnecessary to plan future facilities and areas exactly. If one kind of facility is inadequate, some of the demand can often be diverted to another type of facility which is relatively larger, for instance. Adjustments in demand and in use are possible. On the other hand, there are real limits to this sort of adjustment. It may well result in a perversion of the use of one kind of area, to less important use than it is suited for, or to a heavier use than its capacity can accommodate.

POLICY ISSUES

This chapter has raised several issues of public policy. How much land and water do we need, properly to meet probable future demands for outdoor recreation? In considering this question, the quality aspect of outdoor recreation should be kept strongly in mind. The question can be rephrased: how crowded do we went our outdoor recreation areas to be? These questions are only partly economic. One can estimate, subject to considerable error, probable future demand for outdoor recreation, under anticipated population, income, leisure, and other conditions. But conversion of these demands to area requires some idea of desirable use standards, and this in turn must be based largely upon what people want, and are willing to pay for.

Can the nation afford the land and water resources required to provide outdoor recreation at a desired level? We have suggested that it can; others may not agree. Again, the problem is only partly economic. We can estimate, subject to some error, the probable economic return to the nation if resources are used for recreation instead of other uses. But we may not all accept the answer; if recreation returns more than other uses, some will still argue that recreation is not essential, that food and fiber are; or others will argue that recreation is too important to be neglected even if its economic return is less. Whatever the resource situation, can the nation afford the money that adequate recreation will cost? We think that it can, but others may not agree. One reason why the demand for outdoor recreation is so high is that average incomes are rising; why cannot part of the increased income be used to provide the recreation sought? The capacity to pay may exist, but the institutional mechanism through which this capacity might be translated into actual expenditures may be inadequate. Specifically, how shall the necessary public funds be raised—by general taxes, by revenue bonds, through special taxes, or by entrance fees? This is an issue to which we shall return in more detail in Chapter VII.

How can we encourage greater public use of private land and water for outdoor recreation? Perhaps a prior question is, should we not acquire more specific knowledge than we now have, as to present use and possible future use of private resources for this purpose? Almost everyone agrees that it would be desirable to have greater use of private resources for outdoor recreation; after all, by far the greater part of the total land area is privately owned. But this seems to be an instance where everyone is for virtue and against sin, without anyone being willing to do very much specifically to bring about what we all agree is desirable. What specific, practical steps might be taken to encourage private landowners to make their lands more generally available for public recreation use?

5

PUBLIC AND PRIVATE
EFFORTS TO PROVIDE
OUTDOOR RECREATION

    OUTDOOR RECREATION HAS ALWAYS BEEN PRO-
vided by both public and private efforts, in varying degrees and
in several ways. This is true if we focus only upon the provision
of the actual site for outdoor recreation; in Chapter IV, we gave
some data on the areas and uses of land in various kinds of public
ownership and also pointed to the serious deficiency in data for
use of privately owned lands. However, as we noted in Chapter III,
the activities at the recreation site itself are but one of five major
phases of the whole outdoor recreation experience; and public and
private efforts are intermingled in each of the other phases as well.

    In the planning or anticipation phase of the experience, the
recreationist utilizes information from both public and private
sources. He gets maps, leaflets, booklets, and other printed information, and sometimes supplements this by discussions with em-

ployees of public and private organizations. He buys equipment from private manufacturers and sellers, but these in turn have often benefited greatly by publicly supported research efforts. His travel to the recreation site is typically in an auto manufactured by private business, using gasoline also provided by private enterprise; but he travels over roads publicly built and maintained. The same is true, of course, for his travel back from the recreation site, to his home. Lastly, in the recollection phase of the whole experience, he relies upon snapshots taken with privately made and sold film but also often upon the same kinds of publicly provided information materials that he used in the planning phase. Thus we find that in each major phase of the whole experience, to varying degrees, the recreationist uses both publicly and privately provided goods and services. This interdependence of public and private effort characterizes the American economy and culture in many ways, but it is seldom more evident than with outdoor recreation.

In the foregoing paragraph, we have mentioned public efforts in the recreation field as though they had a unity or singleness of origin. In fact, however, public efforts in the recreation field are highly diverse and scattered in themselves. Table 2 illustrates this

TABLE 2

GOVERNMENT AGENCIES AND FUNCTIONS RELATING TO
OUTDOOR RECREATION AREAS

Government Branch or Agency	General Functions
Federal Government (one)	
Congress	Passes laws, makes appropriations, investigates
President	General direction of Executive Branch
Department of Agriculture	Directs agricultural and forestry programs
Forest Service	Manages national forests
Department of the Interior	Directs various resource programs
National Park Service	Manages national park system
Fish and Wildlife Service	Manages federal wildlife areas
Bureau of Land Management	Manages grazing districts and public domain

TABLE 2 (*cont.*)

Bureau of Reclamation	Builds and operates reservoirs
Bureau of Outdoor Recreation	Coordinates and plans federal recreation
Department of the Army	Has certain civil works responsibilities
Corps of Engineers	Plans and builds flood control and navigation projects
Tennessee Valley Authority	Builds multipurpose water management projects

State Governments
(50)

(Situation differs greatly among states; common situation described here.)

Legislature	Passes laws, makes appropriations, investigates
Governor	General supervision over Executive Branch
Park Board or Department*	Manages state park system
Forestry Board or Department*	Manages state forests
Wildlife Board or Department*	Manages state wildlife refuges
State Highway Department	Manages waysides and other areas along highways

Counties
(about 3,000—most do not have specialized recreation agencies)

Usually have some general governing group, often called commissioners
May have park and/or recreation departments or officers, to manage parks (if any) and to direct activities on playgrounds or other outdoor areas
May manage school systems, including use of playgrounds for general recreation

Cities
(over 4,000 with 2,500 or more population—more than half have specialized recreation agencies)

Generally have mayor, city council, and sometimes appointed general manager
Like counties, may have park departments or officers, recreation directors, and school administration, each of which is concerned with management of particular outdoor recreation areas

*May be an agency independent of the governor.

diversity, at least in part. Provision of some services essential to or useful for outdoor recreation is carried out by government at each of its "levels"—federal, state, county, and city. In the following sections of this chapter, we shall briefly consider the outdoor recreation activities of each of these kinds of government. However, equally important is the fact that government at each level frequently operates through more than one kind of agency; sometimes the different kinds of agencies perform different functions, but sometimes they do closely similar things. Various explanations underlie this seemingly inconsistent pattern; in many instances, only the history of the activity in question, including the role played by key or dominant personalities at various stages, can explain what has arisen.

Similarly, private efforts in the outdoor recreation field are highly diverse. Later in this chapter, we shall try to describe some of them; but information here is not as general as for public agencies.

Before looking at each level of government and at the private efforts, it may be helpful merely to list the activities in regard to outdoor recreation that are, or might be, performed at different levels or places. First of all, there is recreation planning; estimation of recreation demand, translation of demand into land and water area, specification of locational requirements, general management plans, and the like. Another major function, almost wholly neglected in the past but likely to increase greatly in importance in the future, is research and the provision of basic data. In this modern complex and technical world, no human activity can be carried on with tolerable competence unless it is underpinned with competent research. Thirdly, there is provision of the outdoor recreation areas themselves; although often thought of as the only function, this is but one of several. Lastly, there is the provision of various necessary services in connection with the use of the areas. Recreation leadership is the most obvious, but not the only one. Supervision over health and safety standards is another necessary service. These various kinds of services may all be performed for a particular area by a single public agency or private group; or they may be divided among several agencies or organizations.

ROLE OF FEDERAL GOVERNMENT

The federal government has traditionally supplied the major resource-based, publicly owned outdoor recreation areas in the United States.

The various kinds of units in the national park system (national parks, national monuments, historical areas, etc.), the national forests, and the federal wildlife refuges have mostly fitted into this category. Their area and use were described in Chapter IV, and need not be repeated here. In addition, the reservoirs and surrounding areas provided by the Corps of Engineers and by the Tennessee Valley Authority have been classed by us as intermediate areas, and also described in Chapter IV. These agencies have not only provided their respective areas, but have improved them for use by the public, to the degree that was deemed appropriate or that was possible with available funds. Moreover, they have provided such services to the recreationists as were available at these sites. In the case of museums and some kinds of historical areas, guide or "interpretation" services have been available, not only to help the recreationists but also to protect the sites as well. These federal agencies have typically provided certain data regarding these areas, such as numbers of visitors; but these data have so often been in the form of mimeographed releases or such other relatively impermanent forms of publication that libraries have not been able to classify and save them, so that in fact such data have not been available to many potential users without disproportionate effort.

Federal agencies have provided other services, to varying degrees. Each agency has done a certain amount of planning on its own lands, although until a decade or so ago this was often on a rather superficial basis. The National Park Service has done some general planning in cooperation with state agencies. Although its efforts in this direction have been carried on for about 25 years, they have been only moderately effective, in part because of lack of funds. Very little research on outdoor recreation has been done by federal agencies. The Forest Service has had authority to do such research, and some limited funds, but its activities in this field have been modest and recent. The other research agencies of the Department of Agriculture have done a little research, particularly on private activities in outdoor recreation, but their efforts have also been rather small and recent.

The Public Health Service has given technical help to the federal and state recreation agencies on health matters, particularly water supply and sewage disposal for recreation areas, and also on safety matters. The Agricultural Extension Service has worked with similar agencies in the states to provide advice and help to farm groups interested in outdoor recreation for themselves or as a source of income. The federal housing agencies have been concerned with outdoor recreation in the slum clearance and urban renewal programs undertaken in the larger cities. There are other relatively minor ways in which federal agencies have aided in provision of outdoor recreation areas or services.

Within the past few years, the federal government has embarked upon a new range of activities in outdoor recreation. Under the Housing Act of 1954, grants-in-aid are available to cities for comprehensive planning ("701" grants, as they are commonly called, from the relevant section of the Act); this planning can include consideration of open spaces and recreation, as well as of other aspects of city growth and development. Still more recently, under the Housing Act of 1961, federal grants-in-aid are available to cities to help purchase land for open space, including specifically for recreation use. These grants can be for 20 per cent of the land acquisition cost if a single city is involved, but for 30 per cent if a whole metropolitan area is involved. In each case, the open space purchased must fit into an over-all plan for the region.

The federal government in 1959 entered the outdoor recreation field on a more comprehensive scale and in a new way. In that year, by special legislation, an Outdoor Recreation Resources Review Commission was established, consisting of eight members of Congress and seven members appointed by the President. In the Preface, we called attention to this commission and to its final report. The latter was publicly released in early 1962, and subsequently a long series of study reports was published. The commission itself passed out of existence in September, 1962. This was the most comprehensive look at outdoor recreation in this country, except possibly for a somewhat similar (though privately financed) semigovernmental effort of the early 1920's; that earlier effort produced an impressive tonnage of reports which resulted in very little action and has long since been forgotten by all except specialists in the field. The 1962 report considers future demands for outdoor recreation, the areas of land and water needed to meet those demands, and the public and private programs that will be necessary. It specifically gets into policy issues at federal, state, local, and private levels.

This report had one immediate result. One of its recommendations was for the establishment of a federal Bureau of Outdoor Recreation, in the Department of the Interior. That was done immediately. The new bureau is to collect information, conduct research, do general recreation planning, and coordinate the outdoor recreation activities among federal agencies. The latter function will be difficult to carry out; one bureau is being asked to coordinate the activities of other bureaus, some in the same department and some in other departments, with no real authority over any of them. The new bureau can be effective only to the degree it is able to show real intellectual leadership.

The report of the commission made many other recommendations, one of which was for the establishment of a federal fund for land acquisition, directly by federal agencies or by means of grants-in-aid to states, for park and recreation purposes. Land can often be bought, before need becomes acute, for vastly less money and with much less trouble and turmoil, than later when needs are acute. If such a fund were established under the control of the new bureau, this would greatly strengthen its role in dealing with other federal agencies and with the states. Special taxes and sources of revenue were proposed for this fund. Legislation to implement this recommendation was introduced in the Congress in 1962 but did not pass at that session of Congress. One public policy issue during the next few years will be this recommendation, until the bill is passed or decisively defeated.

Another recommendation of the commission was for a system of federal grants-in-aid to the states, for recreation planning purposes. These grants were proposed for a five-year period, with major

89

federal help at first which would gradually decline during the life of the program. A bill incorporating this proposal was introduced in Congress in 1962 but did not pass that session.

The federal government is also moving to extend the national park system to new areas. Following a period of its rapid extension in the 1930's, relatively few additions were made during the 1940's and 1950's. In 1961, the Cape Cod National Seashore area was authorized, and in 1962 Padre Island in Texas and Point Reyes in California were added. These three are unique in that, for the first time, the federal government is obligated to buy the major part of the lands involved. In earlier extensions, either the land was already federally owned or else it was acquired by private and state interests and donated to the federal government. Proposed extensions of the national park system are as follows:

national parks: Canyonlands, in Utah; Great Basin, in Nevada; and Prairie, in Kansas;

national monuments: Florissant Fossil Beds, in Colorado; Fossil Butte, in Wyoming; Ozark Rivers, in Missouri; Pecos, in New Mexico; and Poverty Point, in Louisiana;

national recreation areas: Allagash, in Maine; Between-the-Lakes, in Kentucky and Tennessee; Tocks Island, in New Jersey and Pennsylvania; and Whiskeytown, in California;

national lakeshores: Indiana Dunes, in Indiana; and Sleeping Bear Dunes, in Michigan;

national seashores: Oregon Dunes, in Oregon; and Pictured Rocks, in Michigan;

scientific reserve: Ice Age, in Wisconsin;

parkways: Allegheny, in Maryland, West Virginia, Virginia, and Kentucky; and George Washington Memorial (extension), in Virginia;

national historical park: Chesapeake and Ohio Canal, in Maryland;

national historic sites: Theodore Roosevelt Birthplace and Saga-more Hill, in New York; Boston, in Massachusetts; Fort Bowie, in Arizona; Fort Larned, in Kansas; Golden Spike, in Utah; Hubbell Trading Post, in Arizona; and Saint-Gaudens, in New Hampshire.

ROLE OF STATES

States provide most of the publicly owned intermediate type of out-door recreation areas, in addition to the federal reservoir areas al-ready discussed. These areas go by many names: state parks are common, but various other designations apply to areas primarily designed for recreation, in the sense we use the term here. There are also state forests, in some states, sometimes state wildlife refuges, sometimes other kinds of natural areas under various names, which provide outdoor recreation in addition to their primary functions; and in most states the highway departments construct and maintain waysides, rest stops, and other kinds of areas along highways which are particularly useful to the traveller. Data on numbers, area, and use of the primary recreation areas are given in Chapter IV and need not be repeated; data on the other kinds of areas are scattered or nonexistent.

States administer these areas in highly varied ways. Much greater use is made of the citizen board, either in an advisory capac-ity, or as a policy-making body, or even in direct administration, than is true of the federal agencies. Such boards are often able to tap the interest and expertise of citizens who would be unwilling to take full-time employment from the state. In this respect, they are excellent; in other ways, they are often less good. For one thing, the members of such boards are often unwilling or unable to devote enough time to the public business to do it justice; sometimes its members represent very special interests, not the general public in-terest; and sometimes such boards are primarily sources of personal

prestige and power, rather than of service. States tend also to frag-
ment the administration of their recreation areas; special boards or
organizations often exist for particular areas. This is true in New
York State, for instance, where there are no less than nine special
recreation administering bodies or boards. When account is taken
of the forest and other kinds of areas on which recreation is allowed,
it appears that, in general, state administration is at least as badly
fragmented as is federal recreation resource administration.

By and large, the state agencies administering areas for recreation supply whatever services are available to recreationists on
the same areas. State health and other specialized services provide
their special programs on state as on federal areas.

States have been woefully weak in recreation planning; much
of what has been done at the state level has been in response to im-
petus provided by federal agencies. This was particularly true during
the 1930's, when federal funds granted to states made possible park
and recreation planning for the first time in many states. The state
park agencies have, until recently, typically not developed long-range
plans, even for their own programs and most certainly not for all
outdoor recreation in their state. Within the past five years, a few
states have made notable advances in this regard. California set up
a special state-wide recreation planning program, that resulted in a
two-volume report of unusual breadth and competence. New York,
Massachusetts, New Jersey, Pennsylvania, Michigan, Wisconsin, Utah,
Nevada, and Washington—to name the more obvious ones—has each
produced some sort of state-wide outdoor recreation or park plan
and program, in greater or less detail and competence. However,
these states have been the exception; in most states there has been
no over-all, long-range planning of outdoor recreation. Moreover,
even in the states named the efforts have typically been one-shot
affairs, with no provision for regular systematic revision and follow-up.

Research on outdoor recreation at the state level has been almost
completely nonexistent. The various state agencies administering
outdoor recreation and parks have not been authorized, staffed, or
financed to do research. Their job has been one of administering

areas entrusted to them; they cannot fairly be criticized for not doing what they have not been asked to do. Nevertheless, the lack of research at the state level is serious. It is highly probable that the lack of facts and understanding which can be produced only through research is costing the states heavily, both now and in the future. Wise, timely, economic expansion of state park systems requires research and planning concerning demand, capabilities of different areas, layout and management, and many other aspects; and most efficient administration of the existing areas likewise requires research.

State park systems collect some information regarding the areas they administer, although such information is published primarily by the National Park Service and by private organizations. Even this information is rather limited. Almost no data are collected by state agencies about outdoor recreation in general in their states. Many state agencies publicize estimates of numbers of tourists or recreationists and of expenditures by them, and such figures are often widely quoted; in general, however, they rest on a very slender factual basis and are often based upon fuzzy and ill-defined concepts.

In some states, there is a recreation service agency, as well as various agencies administering state-owned recreation lands. These service agencies provide guidance and technical help to local recreation bodies, and are often of major help to them.

The general weakness of state recreation agencies is the more regrettable, because of the almost certainly larger role of state parks in the future than in the past. As we have noted in Chapter II, user-oriented outdoor recreation areas can satisfy only part of the greatly expanded future demand for outdoor recreation, even if their area expands as much as is desirable; and the resource-based outdoor recreation areas have definite limits on their total use, if their quality is not to be completely destroyed. But intermediate areas, of which state parks are the prime example, can be expanded almost without limit and can provide an increasingly larger part of the total recreation supply in the future. It is noteworthy that the Outdoor Recreation Commission report gave special attention to the problems and possibilities of state park systems. To achieve their potential, however, state park agencies must be much better organized, staffed, and financed than they have been in the past. If the recently proposed legislation, arising out of the commission's studies, for a system of federal grants for state recreation planning should be passed, this would help greatly in strengthening state efforts.

CITIES AND OUTDOOR RECREATION

Counties and special recreation districts also provide outdoor recreation, but their problems and opportunities are so similar to those of cities that they are included here also.

In cities, more than at any other level of government, the difference between parks and recreation, or between resources and activities, becomes clear. That is, all larger cities and most smaller ones have parks of some kind and size; these are areas in which many kinds of activities are carried on, but much of the value of the park comes from the trees, grass, water, and other natural resources, without too intensive human use. At the same time, these cities have playgrounds, playing fields, and numerous other kinds of recreation areas where activities rather than resources are dominant. Every area has some resources and some activity; it is simply that the proportions differ greatly between parks and recreation areas (in the narrower sense). This difference in emphasis often is reflected in a difference in organization; separate park departments and recreation departments are common. It is further emphasized by differences in professional training and experience of personnel. Park managers are likely to have forestry or other resource-oriented training; recreation leaders are likely to have physical education, general education, or specialized recreation training. Each group must concern itself with resources and with activities, but again in very different proportions.

The situation as to number of areas, acreage, and use of urban parks was discussed in Chapter IV and need not be repeated. In general, the oldest, central districts of the larger cities have few parks and recreation areas; all land use is intensive, and this is true for play as for work and living areas. The old but intermediate residential areas sometimes are much better provided for; these are the districts where park programs of earlier decades sometimes resulted in adequate parks. The newer suburbs have often lagged in development of park and recreation area; in part, they have utilized the areas of the older city, in part they have not yet been able to afford the extensions of their own systems.

In cities, there is more tendency for recreation services to be provided by different organizations than manage the areas, than is true for other types of outdoor recreation areas. That is, recreation departments may have active programs on school grounds or in parks, to a degree seldom found with state or federal areas.

In cities, citizen boards for park or recreation management are often used, as at the state level. Most of the comments about state boards apply here also.

Recreation planning by city park and recreation departments has been very weak and often nonexistent. General city planners must take recreation needs, demands, and opportunities into account, in any well-rounded plans that may be developed; and this has been done in many cities. However, such planning has often been weak in its estimation of future recreation demand. There has been an unfortunate gap between the recreation specialists and the general city planners, in many cities.

Recreation research is almost unknown at the city level. Even more than with state organizations, city departments are unequipped to do research, have lacked funds for it, and have not been given the responsibility. Faced with demanding administrative and management problems which have frequently strained their budgets, they have naturally not emphasized research needs. However, as with the states, the results are unfortunate; research in this field, perhaps by specialized research agencies, would almost certainly yield handsome dividends to society.

The urban recreation organizations have often been weak on

data collection and even more on data publication. Such data as exist on urban outdoor recreation have nearly all been collected by a private organization (the National Recreation Association) or by a federal agency (the Bureau of the Census). Data on land area, numbers of buildings, numbers of employees, and some other factors are reasonably good, although reporting has never been complete. On the other hand, data on usage of the available areas and facilities have been poor; in part, this is because it would be difficult to get reliable data on this point, since access to the various areas is so free and informal. However, almost no use has been made of sampling techniques for obtaining data in this field.

Outdoor recreation provided by cities competes more closely with outdoor recreation provided by private groups, which we discuss in the next section, and with activities other than outdoor recreation, than does outdoor recreation at any other level. No individual or small group of individuals can own and operate their private equivalent of a national park, for instance; yet the person or group dissatisfied with public swimming facilities may construct and operate its own. Likewise, viewing TV, going to a movie, or reading a murder mystery may be a more practical substitute for outdoor recreation at the local park or playground than it is for a vacation trip to the beach or to the mountains. The time distribution of leisure, which we discussed in Chapter I, makes some substitutions more feasible than others.

OUTDOOR RECREATION PROVIDED BY PRIVATE GROUPS

Outdoor recreation is provided by a large number and by many kinds of private groups; unfortunately, their number and variety is matched by the lack of information about them. A few are relatively large, with national memberships, but most have a more limited range of activity, and many are strictly local. A few are interested primarily in the relatively extensive types of outdoor recreation, but more are interested in the relatively intensive types, such as swimming, golf, tennis, and horseback riding. Private groups are more likely to be interested in activities than in resources; in this they resemble the city parks and recreation agencies, discussed in the foregoing section.

Few private recreation groups are active in recreation planning, at least beyond the scope of their own (often limited) activities. They are often not interested in planning all recreation activities for their own members, but only those particular activities which brought the group together. There are a few private general planning groups, such as the Regional Plan Association of New York, which have given attention to recreation planning. None, to our knowledge, has conducted research on outdoor recreation. University faculty members, of course, have conducted some research on various aspects of outdoor recreation, and these may be considered private groups in one sense of the word. But the private recreation associations have not been in the research business. Neither have they been in the data-gathering business; it is a major research project, like as not to end in failure, to ascertain how many members a particular organization has had annually for the past ten years; and to find out how many people it served, and how its services related to those of other private or public organizations, is more than can be found out in most circumstances.

Some private organizations provide recreation areas for their members. There is an unknown but presumably fairly large number of cooperative swimming pool associations, for instance; there are several hundred country clubs and golf or tennis clubs, some providing a range of services beyond their specialty. In some instances, organizations such as the Izaak Walton League own land and facilities locally for their members.

More commonly, private recreation groups provide services for their members, not only on owned areas but also on public areas. The larger regional organizations, such as the Sierra Club and the Mountaineers on the Pacific Coast and the Appalachian Club in the East, do more to provide services than area, although the latter owns some rights over land. The national organizations such as the Audu-

97

bon Society and the National Wildlife Federation provide some services, mostly information, to their members. The same is true of the National Parks Association and of the Wilderness Society. A major citizen group concerned with recreation, especially user-oriented recreation, is the National Recreation Association. Some of these organizations are not strictly recreational; they are perhaps more conservational, but they do have recreational importance. One of their greatest services to their members is a watchdog role over public actions, and as an influence on public action in directions desirable to them. In a democracy, where public action is nearly always to some extent a compromise between divergent and even contending forces, each group has both a right and a duty to represent its members. These organized private groups are thus an important part of our functioning democracy. In addition, there are several organizations of professional personnel working in this field—the American Recreation Society, the Conference on State Parks, the American Institute of Park Executives, and others.

Private recreation groups perform other major functions as well. For one thing, they provide a safety valve for those persons who are dissatisfied with public programs. They enable groups with common interests to associate together, free of distraction from other groups. This may sometimes serve to perpetuate racial, social, income, or other distinctions which from a broader viewpoint it might be desirable to see diminished. But the existence of the private alternatives may make public action easier to accomplish—abolishment of racial discrimination at public swimming pools, for instance.

Although data are lacking, it appears highly probable that the private recreation groups serve a selected membership, as far as socio-economic characteristics are concerned. While very rich people may have their own swimming pool, they are likely to belong to an exclusive country club for their golf; moderate income people may belong to a cooperative swimming pool, but low income ones are most unlikely to do so. It is not only that capital investment and annual operating costs are involved, but the lower income groups often lack the kind of public leadership which can organize such undertakings.

The effect of private recreation groups is thus probably to widen the already considerable disparity in availability of outdoor recreation areas that we noted for public areas. The poorer people live where public recreation is less, and they are least likely to have private groups to provide their own.

RECREATION RESEARCH AND PLANNING

In this chapter we have made several references to research and planning for outdoor recreation. A more explicit, but still relatively brief, treatment of these subjects now seems worth while.

First of all, we need to consider what we mean by "research." As used here, the word means an organized search for knowledge, particularly as to causes and relationships, from which a synthesis of known facts and concepts can be developed, and which will lead to wider valid generalizations. As such, research supplements common experience. For instance, in agriculture, farmers over the centuries in many lands have learned how to grow crops and raise livestock, sometimes with great skill. But farmers typically have not understood the basic scientific facts of plant growth, genetics, nutrition, and the like. They have frequently assigned wrong reasons or causes to observable phenomena, and have assumed that relationships existed everywhere which in fact were peculiar to a certain place and time. As a result, they have often been unable to deal with new problems which would arise in their familiar surroundings, or would be unable to deal with a new environment. Generations of research in agriculture have gradually uncovered basic reasons and led to an understanding of observable processes; this in turn has led to the formulation of "laws," or generalizations of wider scope than the observed facts; and this in time has led to an immense amount of applied research, directly applicable to agricultural problems. Our knowledge of basic processes is yet far from complete; for instance, we are only beginning to understand the fundamental chemistry of heredity, or the basic process of photosynthesis.

99

Research is often broadly grouped into basic or pure, and applied. The first seeks to uncover the laws, processes, and principles by which some activity proceeds. The second is directed to specific problems or situations. In practice, the line between pure and applied research is not sharp and clear, but rather one shades into the other.

In outdoor recreation, administrators, supporters of recreation, users of recreation areas, legislators, and others have developed considerable knowledge, based upon their personal experiences. Considering how short is the period of organized outdoor recreation, compared to agriculture, for instance, the accumulation of knowledge is relatively great. An experienced person can estimate or guess the volume of usage of a new recreation area, or can estimate the capacity of a given area to provide a particular kind of outdoor recreation, often with considerable accuracy. But this kind of knowledge, accumulated from experience, is far different from the kind of knowledge that can be built up by research. There has been almost no basic research applied to outdoor recreation. Anyone familiar with outdoor recreation development and administration realizes that a recreation area creates economic values; the fact that so many people wish to use it, often at considerable expense to themselves, is one evidence of this. Any administrator who has proposed closing a park, and has encountered the protests of the public, knows this also. Yet the basic principles of how economic values are created by outdoor recreation, where they arise, who gets them, and similar matters have had almost no study. The need is acute for basic research, to develop principles, understanding, and laws, not only for this but also for other aspects of outdoor recreation. There is equally great need for research applied to specific areas and problems, but the latter is likely to be relatively unproductive until a better theoretical framework has been developed.

In agriculture, in the last generation the total output has doubled, from a slightly smaller crop area, with only half as much labor as formerly, and with only slightly more capital. Agriculture is in the midst of a technological revolution, which has just begun its major transformation. This technological change rests upon a large and long-continued program of research.

100

Outdoor recreation must cope with a steadily mounting demand, over the next several decades. This rising demand will require large new areas of land and water for outdoor recreation, much more capital investment for this purpose, more manpower in managing the areas, and a much larger total output of recreation services and values. The total values created by outdoor recreation are a major fraction of those created by agriculture, for instance, yet the amount of research in outdoor recreation is minuscule as compared with agriculture. There is every reason to believe that research applied to outdoor recreation can be as productive as has been research applied to agriculture.

Organized research may be conducted by specialized research institutions, or by organizations primarily engaged in management of outdoor recreation areas or activities, or by both. In the case of agriculture, research is carried out in land grant colleges located in each state, and also by the United States Department of Agriculture. A specialized research agency, separated from the pressures of operating decisions, can perhaps conduct basic research better—the atmosphere is quieter, and there are fewer pressures to affect the results. On the other hand, an organization actually engaged in various programs sometimes understands better what the problems are, and what may practically be done about them. In the case of outdoor recreation, some research might appropriately be carried out by park and forest managing agencies, and some by colleges and universities. It seems probable that most research in this field will be publicly supported, especially the basic research. Yet, as in agriculture, there may well be some privately financed or privately organized research of an applied nature.

By "planning," we mean the assembly and the ordering of all available relevant facts, to the end of formulating a scheme of action. Planning rests upon research. If the latter is deficient, the planners may be forced into doing a certain amount of research themselves; this is generally unsatisfactory, because the research has to be too hurried and circumscribed and because the planning is likely to still have too meager a research base. Planning, for outdoor recreation or any other purpose, should include a wide enough area and a long enough time span to meet the situation adequately. In practice, of course, it is not always easy to know how large an area or how long a time span to include.

Planning for outdoor recreation suffers several severe handicaps. In the first place, as we have noted in this chapter, the responsibility for outdoor recreation is fragmented among many governmental agencies at all levels of government, and among numerous private organizations as well. Yet, for each agency and organization, an important consideration in formulating its plans is the plans and programs of the other agencies and organizations; none can decide alone, without considering the others. In the second place, immediate operating programs have been highly demanding of outdoor recreation agencies, and there has been a notable lack of a long-term outlook. Legislative and appropriating bodies have not encouraged outdoor recreation managing agencies to look ahead, and often they have not provided the necessary funds for making such plans. In the third place, there has been a serious lack of agreed-upon standards for outdoor recreation, and of adequate measures of the value of recreation. The agencies concerned have had to present plans and proposals which often rested primarily upon personal judgments and personal standards of value.

Good planning for outdoor recreation would accomplish several results: it would insure that there is enough outdoor recreation area, when and where needed, to meet the demands; it would minimize the costs of providing such needed areas; it would increase user satisfactions from the areas available; and it would greatly reduce duplication of effort and waste in providing outdoor recreation opportunity.

POLICY ISSUES

The existence of outdoor recreation programs at each major level of government, usually with a multiplicity of programs at each level, and the numerous private organizations active in the general field, all raise a number of policy issues.

First of all, how may it be possible to get coordinated recreation planning, given this multiplicity and variety of organizations? It is most unlikely that plans will be well coordinated, with neither serious gaps nor expensive duplication, in the absence of some formal means of coordination. It can be argued that private productive activities are coordinated through the operation of the competitive market (it can also be argued that such coordination is inherently wasteful); but in recreation, where neither the services produced nor the required resources are bought and sold in a market which is a competitive one in the faintest degree, such a mechanism of coordination is absent. Governmental affairs, not subject to the usual market price restraints, require coordination in other ways. How might this best be done? One "solution" would be to require highly centralized control over all public recreation planning; this approach would almost surely be rejected in the United States, for we have usually opposed centralized power in the absence of an emergency such as war; and, in any event, this might create as many problems as it "solved." The issue thus may be rephrased: how may we get coordinated but not centralized recreation planning?

No single, simple answer seems possible. Various coordinating councils or boards might be set up, at metropolitan, state, and federal levels, which could advise and bring some gentle pressures but not compel. Such mechanisms do in fact exist, in some states and places; their influence to date has been modest. The growth of grants-in-aid, from federal to state and city governments, and from states to cities and counties, could certainly bring a large measure of coordination. By persistently asking, how does this proposal fit with those of other organizations in your area? the agency making the grants could exert a major influence. While this would be a measure of central control, yet the fact that it was a necessary prelude to a grant of funds might make it more acceptable to the recipients. General budgeting agencies, in government and in private fund organizations such as Community Chests, could also exert some influence. An informed public, which also raised similar questions about both government and private recreation efforts, could also be effective.

Perhaps an even more basic question is: what is the proper role of government at each level, in providing public recreation? Should the federal government limit itself to provision of only some types of outdoor recreation, or only to provision of funds to states and municipalities, so that they may provide recreation; and similarly for other levels of government? The present multiplicity of activities—the general "untidiness" of the whole situation—may suggest a more drastic remedy to some. As we have noted, there is some tendency for specialization of functions now, but a most incomplete one; the national parks and national forests provide types of recreation not usually found in city parks, for example; but there is a considerable overlap in activities between federal and state areas, and between state and municipal areas. Recreation activities at various levels, as indeed most other governmental activities, arose to meet a need and a demand by the public. The various programs may not have been the most rational, given all the circumstances; but they certainly had a sufficient measure of public support to come into being and to persist.

This suggests that major revision of responsibility of governments at different levels, to evolve a cleaner, neater division of labor among them as far as outdoor recreation is concerned, is unlikely. Indeed, the trend is likely to be the reverse—more involvement of government at each level in activities once thought to be appropriate only to other levels of government. If this is thought undesirable, it must be resisted; if thought inevitable, it makes more important than before the need for coordination through some mechanism such as we have discussed above. Coordination may be necessary not only in planning, but in operation also.

Can the governmental structure at each major level be simplified and coordinated? In particular, can the number of agencies providing outdoor recreation in some manner be reduced? More specifically, can state park, forest, conservation, fish and game, and possibly other agencies be brought into one large agency (with subdivisions) and thus be brought better into coordination? At the federal level, can all the resource-administering agencies be brought into one department, possibly with recreation under some form of central direction?

In the cities, can the recreation, parks, and perhaps other departments or units be combined? Moves of this kind have a certain appeal, especially to persons concerned with a single major form of activity; they also raise major questions. These agencies each have a certain clientele; each was created and persists to perform a particular function or functions; their very existence is proof of a certain strength, probably of a resistance to merger or extermination. Some moves in this direction have been made at the federal level—we have noted the creation of the new Bureau of Outdoor Recreation—and at the state level—some states have established major departments of natural resources within which parks and recreation are often located. More might be done, and perhaps will be; but resistance is likely to be great, and success achieved only under a strong political leader with a positive program.

Might it in fact be undesirable to have carefully centralized and controlled recreation activities at each major level of government? Are there positive advantages in a multiplicity of agencies? Does a measure of competition among them provide the citizen with better service and less likelihood of governmental domination? Are some possible efficiencies in use of funds through centralization of programs important enough to warrant establishing what will or might be a powerful government agency monopoly control over citizens?

6

ECONOMIC VALUES CREATED
BY OUTDOOR RECREATION

ANY HUMAN ACTIVITY THAT INVOLVES AS MANY people, in as many physical observable activities, as does outdoor recreation, has significant economic consequences. Almost everyone familiar with outdoor recreation will agree to such a statement, but definition and measurement of the economic consequences have been less satisfactory and less unanimous. There are several reasons why this should be so. In the first place, attention has nearly always focused on activities at the recreation site; as we pointed out in Chapter III, this is only one part of the total recreation experience, and often a minor part at that. In the second place, since entrance to outdoor recreation places has traditionally been free or nearly so, many people have found it impossible to realize that large economic values were involved.

The purpose of this chapter is to provide some suggestion as to the total sums involved, for what they are spent, who receives them, and what values are created in the process. At the end, some questions are raised and some policy issues posed.

EXPENDITURES

We noted in Chapter III that money costs are almost always involved in the whole recreation experience, especially at intermediate and resource-based areas. Time and travel costs are also involved, but in this chapter we shall ignore them. Some of the money costs are immediate and direct—money for gasoline for the car, or for purchase of a fishing license, or for any one of scores of other purposes. Some of the money costs are for equipment or durable goods that will be useful for later outdoor recreation experiences—the purchase of a new tent, or of an outboard motor, or of any other specialized recreation equipment. Some costs will be for purchase of a new automobile or as a deferred cost of replacement of the present car; this item of equipment is as nearly all-purpose as one can imagine, yet outdoor recreation often provides one major incentive for car ownership. Some of the money will be spent in the recreationist's home town, before he leaves or after he returns; some will be spent en route to or from the recreation area; and some will be spent in or near the latter.

Several sample studies have been made of expenditures by tourists, travellers, or recreationists. Although these three groups are somewhat different, they are in considerable part the same people viewed in different ways. These studies have often employed different definitions and methodology, so that results are not completely comparable; and they have usually focused only upon cash expenditures and usually upon such expenditures in the neighborhood of the recreation area. However, based upon these studies and upon other information about recreation use of various kinds of areas, some estimates can be made of total expenditures to various kinds of public outdoor recreation areas.

The average visitor to a state park is estimated to have spent

107

$4.50 in cash per person per day, for this kind of recreation. Of this, $2.00 was for food, half in the form of groceries and half in the form of restaurant meals; $.50 was for lodging (only a small percentage of

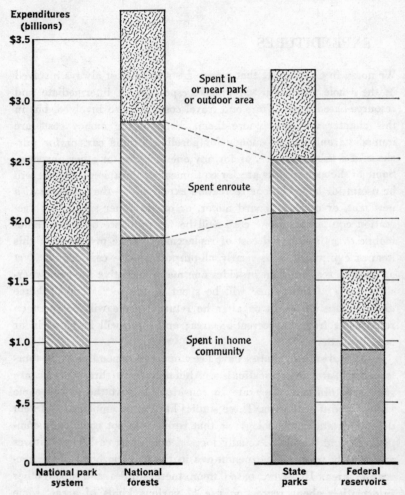

Figure 12. Visitors' expenditures when using four kinds of public outdoor recreation areas in 1960 can be classified according to the amount spent in the home community, en route, and in or near the recreation area.

such visitors had any expense for this purpose, but the costs were naturally much higher for those who stayed overnight) ; $1.00 was for gasoline and oil (total expenditures for this purpose were higher, of course, but also provided transportation for the whole family) ; and the remainder was for various miscellaneous purposes. In addition to the cash costs, each visit involved a charge of $3.50 per day for equipment of various kinds, mostly for the use of the family auto. The total cost per day per visitor is thus estimated at $8.00.

Estimates were made for other kinds of public areas also, but need not be presented in detail. In general, costs per day are higher as the distance to the recreation area is greater and as longer times are spent away from home. The average visit to a national park is estimated to cost $10.00 per person per day in cash, for instance; food costs per day in this case are higher than for state parks, because more meals are eaten away from home and more in restaurants; lodging costs are much higher, because more nights are spent away from home; and direct cash transportation costs are higher, because more miles are travelled each day. In addition, indirect or deferred equipment costs are much higher, partly because equipment is used more and partly because somewhat better equipment is involved. The total cost per visit per day is $15.50, or nearly double that at a state park; and since many more days are involved in the typical visit to a national park, total costs for the whole experience are several times higher.

Estimates have been made for other intermediate and resource-based public recreation areas, which fall between the relatively low figure for state parks and the relatively high figure for national parks. These per-day costs can be multiplied by the number of visits to each type of area and by the number of days an average visit is estimated to require, to get a total national expenditure for these types of outdoor recreation. For 1960, the total was slightly in excess of $11 billion (Figure 12). The largest item was for visits to national forests; a combination of many visits, for comparatively long periods, involving moderately long travel, accounted for a total of $3.7 billion. The next largest item was for visits to state parks, $3.2 billion; al-

though costs per visit were less and length of travel also less, a much
larger number of visits resulted in this large total expenditure. The
national park system was third, with estimated total expenditures of
$2.5 billion. Other kinds of areas were less.

These expenditures have been estimated also according to purpose and place (Figure 13). The largest single item was for use of
the auto—$3.1 billion; next was $1.6 billion for operation of the auto

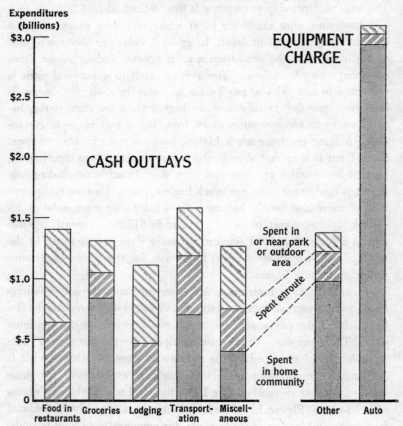

Figure 13. Showing how the recreationists' expenditures in 1960 were dis-
tributed among goods and services purchased at home, en route, and in or near
the public recreation areas visited.

(gasoline, oil, etc.). Other equipment, besides the auto, accounted for $1.4 billion; food in restaurants for $1.4 billion; groceries for $1.3 billion; lodging for $1.1 billion; and other items for the rest. Of the total expenditures for all purposes, more than half was spent in the home community of the recreationist. This was because nearly all the expenditure for equipment purchase and replacement was in the home town; but almost half of the gas and oil was bought there also—the typical recreationist "fills 'er up" before he leaves and after he returns, and for shorter trips buys none elsewhere; and well over half of the groceries purchased came from the home town also. About one-fourth of all the expenditures were in or near the recreation area; expenditures for lodging and for meals in restaurants were particularly large here. Somewhat less than one-fourth was spent en route to and from the recreation area; the typical travel items of restaurant food, lodging, and gas and oil are comparatively large here.

A few observations about these data are in order, to avoid misunderstanding as to their meaning. First of all, they are gross or total expenditures; while they do create profits, jobs, and values, which we consider in more detail in the next section of this chapter, much of the total is spent for services or goods produced elsewhere. The gasoline service station operator, for instance, must buy his gasoline from a wholesaler, who in turn gets it (perhaps indirectly) from a refinery, which got its raw petroleum from a well; and all of this may be located a long distance away from the spot where the recreationist bought his gas. In the second place, these total expenditures are not a net addition to the national volume of business; had the people concerned not made their trips, they would have spent most or all of the money for something else. Most of the groceries purchased would have been bought had the family stayed home; perhaps not as much gasoline would have been bought, but an equivalent sum would have been spent for something else. This latter characteristic is not peculiar to outdoor recreation; the same could be said about movies, television, or even about expenditures for furniture—if the money had not been spent on these, it would have mostly been spent on something. Except for savings and investment, all current income

111

is spent for consumption goods and services of some kind—some homespun philosopher has said that the cost of living never changes, because it is all you make, all the time. Gross expenditure data have their value, if carefully interpreted, but one must be careful not to assume they are net, either to the recipient or to the total economy. Moreover, expenditures in one place or region often merely replace expenditures elsewhere; what is new business to one locality may be lost business to another.

RECREATION EXPENDITURES CREATE JOBS AND BUSINESS

Recreation expenditures of the type just described create jobs and business; the recreationist's cost becomes the businessman's gross income. As we have noted, much of this money turnover must be used to buy goods or services which the retailer sells to the recreationist. Some, however, is a reward to the retail businessman or service man, for the managerial ability, labor, and capital he puts into the business. This is "value added" by his service.

Unfortunately, we lack detailed specific information on the uses to which the recreationist's expenditures are put by the businessmen who receive them. On the basis of general relationships in retail trade, some estimates can be made. For instance, of total expenditures made for meals in restaurants, 52 per cent goes for various kinds of goods (including food, but not limited to it) purchased from other suppliers; 8 per cent is for the owner's compensation; 20 per cent is for labor entering directly into the service; and 20 per cent is for a wide variety of other outlays, including taxes paid. For groceries bought by recreationists, 85 per cent is for supplies the retailer buys from others, with correspondingly smaller shares to the other recipients. At the other extreme is lodging: here, only 25 per cent is for supplies, with 15 per cent to the owners of the business, 30 per cent to workers hired, and 30 per cent for miscellaneous outlays. Most other recreationist expenditures lie between these extremes. The equipment purchased, especially the autos, involves large expenditures for supplies—in this case, for the autos and other equipment purchased from the manufacturer or his representative.

The foregoing relates to the direct expenditures by the recreationist—the first transaction in a chain. The money the recreation supplier spends for supplies in turn becomes gross income to the persons who receive it, and they in turn employ people, pay wages, make profits and return to capital, pay taxes, and the like. The workers to whom the first supplier pays wages also use this income to buy many commodities and services—including in some instances outdoor recreation. The recreationist buys gasoline from the local service station; most of the money the latter pays out goes to the petroleum wholesaler, but some goes as wages, some is for his own return, and so on; and the service station employee in turn buys groceries, gasoline, and countless other goods and services.

If one looks at the whole national economy, nearly all the expenditures represent income to some other person or group; the money flows round and round, each transaction buying goods or services of the same value (Figure 14). For a local or regional economy, however, much of the expenditure is made for goods or services from other localities or regions. As nearly as we can estimate, 45 per cent of total expenditures for outdoor recreation (as described in the foregoing section) are spent for goods and services provided within the locality where the money is first spent by the recreationist; and thus 55 per cent is spent for goods and services from other localities. Although precise data are lacking, we may estimate as a first approximation that 45 per cent of the 45 per cent is in turn spent within the local community by its recipients; and that in turn, 45 per cent of the 45 per cent of the 45 per cent is spent there by the recipients of the second round of expenditures; and so on. The original expenditures are like a large stone dropped in a placid pool; they set up waves, which in turn set up waves, and so on, each successive set of waves weaker than the previous one, until at last the effects are imperceptible. Limiting ourselves to the first three rounds of expenditures locally, it would appear that the

113

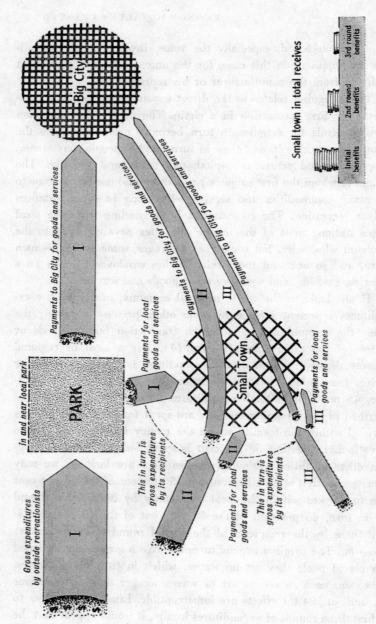

Figure 14. Hypothetical circulation of expenditures for outdoor recreation in a local area.

114

total local impact was equal to roughly 75 per cent of the initial recreationist's expenditures.

On the basis of these data and of national average earnings per employed worker, it appears that the wages paid directly out of the recreationist's expenditures for these public intermediate and resource-based areas would create the equivalent of approximately 200,000 jobs on a full-time year-round basis. Since some of them, at least, were seasonal, the total number of jobs was larger than this. With the multiplier effect previously described, this would mean the equivalent of a total of nearer 400,000 full-time year-round local jobs due to these kinds of outdoor recreation; in addition, of course, much larger numbers of jobs would exist in equipment and other factories which supplied goods for recreation suppliers. In addition, the owner-managers of many of the recreation supply enterprises also had employment. These employment equivalents are to be compared with a total national labor force of over 60 million. While outdoor recreation provides jobs directly, and even more jobs indirectly, it is not a major employer and is not likely to be.

Part of these expenditures at every level go to pay taxes—local property taxes, income taxes, franchise taxes, and various other varieties. At the same time, the people employed in providing these various services require and consume public services of all kinds—schools for their children, roads and streets, water supply and sewerage, general governmental functions, and others. It is impossible, without careful analysis of local situations, to determine whether the taxes so paid are larger or smaller than the cost of the services demanded and used by those paying the taxes. Where recreation travel and tourist business is the chief economic support of an area, then obviously—one way or another—the taxes paid out of visitor expenditures must nearly equal the value of the governmental services consumed by those concerned. Where visitor expenditures are less, relative to the total economy, the taxes may either exceed or fall short of the costs.

As a result of all this business activity, property values rise in the areas where money is spent by the recreationist or by his suppliers. The service station operator whose chief business is supplying

115

tourists and other visitors may develop a valuable business which basically owes its existence to the "outside" money spent there. The same is true, in varying degree, of other businesses serving visitors. Moreover, the value of the home of a businessman whose primary business is serving tourists or recreationists also depends very largely on the profitability of this business. Sometimes, as in the case of the service station mentioned, the recreation basis of the value in the business may be obvious to all concerned. At other times, as in the case of the automobile dealer in the recreationist's home town, the origins of value for his business may be less obvious. The manufacturer of water skis or other specialized recreation equipment may realize that the value of his business arises entirely out of outdoor recreation; this may not be as clear to the auto manufacturer. The more remote a business is, either geographically or in the chain of supply of goods and services, the less obvious is the connection between business value and outdoor recreation.

In addition to the values arising in the various supply businesses, other capital values arise in the recreation property itself. When this is all public, the values may not be obvious, and in fact may have been siphoned off by various private businesses. When private land either provides some of the services or lies around or adjacent to the public recreation area, then some value increases arise on this private property itself. This is a matter we shall explore in more detail in the following section.

WHO GETS THESE NEW VALUES AND WHAT ARE THEIR INTERESTS?

As we have noted, outdoor recreation creates many economic values. These values are dispersed, both as between recipients and geographically. Moreover, some of them are unrecognized by their recipients; and the values created are not necessarily in strict proportion to the volumes of business arising from outdoor recreation. Let us look at these propositions in illustrative terms.

The data we have presented as to expenditures made in visiting federal and state outdoor areas of the resource-based and intermediate types demonstrate how far the gross expenditures are dispersed, between suppliers and among areas. The grocer, the restaurant keeper, the hotel and motel operator, the gasoline service station, the automobile dealer, the sports shop, and many other suppliers each get a part of the recreationist's dollar. Much is spent in the recreationist's home town but other sums are spent in all the towns en route to and near where he is going. The sports shop which sells fishing tackle or outboard motors should readily realize that the source of its business is the outdoor recreationist. So may the motel and hotel keeper, and the restaurateur. But the grocer may be less aware of this fact, and also the automobile dealer. They may make a sales pitch to the recreationist, even to stocking goods or varieties that he specially wants; but the recreationist often looks like any other customer, and it may be hard indeed to know the extent to which a particular business is dependent upon this trade.

Even if a particular business knows exactly the share of its total trade that is with recreationists, this may not show the proportion of its profits and of its business values that are due to the same source. Sometimes a relatively small additional volume of business adds to profits, and hence to business values, disproportionately. That is, more business can sometimes be handled without any significant addition to investment or to labor force; a considerable share of the additional gross income is also net income. A sports equipment shop in a town may get a substantial economic shot in the arm by the addition of a new lake within a few miles, for instance; people now buy more boats, motors, tackle, and other items than previously, which he can sell from his same store with the same labor force. On the other hand, sometimes an expanding field of activity attracts so many new businesses to it that none profit. In this same example, a new sports equipment shop might open up in the same town; now, the slightly larger volume of business must be divided between two stores, and neither may make any real profit. It seems highly probable that in some areas something like this has happened with boats;

117

attracted by the boom in boating, more manufacturers or dealers have sprung up than could expect profitable business.

As we have also noted, one rather clear evidence of the economic values created by outdoor recreation is the value of property around the public outdoor recreation areas. This has been notable in a number of reservoirs built by public agencies. These values are undeniable and may be relatively large. In some cases, the benefits to private property holders are equal to a significant proportion of the total costs of the reservoir. Yet in most cases it is probable that they are but a small fraction of the total values created by the reservoir—they are simply the most obvious. Sometimes the same thing may happen to private land values in an area made more accessible by public expenditures for roads. As a result of the greater accessibility, the land now has greater value for recreation; but, again, it is probable that other values were also created by the new road, that are not so obvious.

Thus far we have talked about outdoor recreation as one major activity, and about economic benefits as one large sum. But there may be divergencies of interest among recreationists and among the economic beneficiaries. Many business interests gain most from sheer volume of recreation use; they have an interest in promoting public policies that foster the maximum number of visits. For instance, such businessmen would naturally oppose any entrance fees to recreation areas, since these would reduce total use, at least to some degree. One can probably put the gasoline service stations in this category; they want to sell as much gas as possible. Among the recreationists, some prefer to have the use of available areas limited, because the quality of the recreation experience is then highest to them. The most extreme situation is the wilderness area or the unspoiled natural outdoor area; too much use there tends to lower the quality of the experience to the user. But even on a popular fishing lake or stream, use beyond some optimum level means a lowering of quality. Something analogous may be true among business groups as well. The operator of a luxury motel or hotel, for instance, is not in favor of maximum numbers of users; rather, he wants use by

118

people of income classes and tastes who can afford to patronize him and who will want to do so. This may require discouragement of mass usage. The outdoor recreation market, including its suppliers, it *not* one big undifferentiated market; rather, it is a series of sub-markets, with interests which are sometimes complementary, some-times competitive. All the suppliers in one region may be in favor or advertising this region to outsiders, or of a better road leading into it; but they may differ considerably as to the class of customers, the kind of service, and even the number of customers that are optimum for them.

PROBLEM:
OUTDOOR RECREATION TO BOLSTER
DEPRESSED AREAS?

There are several economically depressed areas in the United States, where outdoor recreation has been proposed by someone as a major economic salvation. Such depressed areas are typically mountainous or other poor farming areas, where the techniques of modern agri-culture are relatively inapplicable and which as a consequence are unable to keep pace with the swiftly changing agricultural times; or they are erstwhile forested areas, now cut over and depleted, with little economic forest output; or they are mining areas which have exhausted their mineral or fuel deposits or can no longer mine them profitably. Such areas exist in the more mountainous districts from New England, down the Appalachian Chain, and across the South; in the Ozarks; in the northern Lake States; and in various other locations around the nation. In almost every case, total population is relatively low in relation to total area; average population density per square mile is low (though perhaps high in relation to resource usability). The low population density leads some people to assume that the area is somehow unused, full of recreation potential, "un-spoiled" in some sense. One is tempted to conclude from some state-ments that any area lacking in any other asset must therefore have

119

recreational value. The possibility of developing outdoor recreation, to attract people from other areas to spend their money here, is a real one, that should by all means be explored. But several cautions or disquieting notes should be sounded.

In the first place, the mere fact that any district or locality is not densely populated does not mean that it has any significant recreation values. There may be no one there because no one wants to go there. Even if it has potential recreation values, in the physical sense, it may be located so far from any large body of potential users that visits to it would be few, no matter what improvements might be made. Moreover, even if large numbers of recreationists can be attracted to a particular district, this does not prove that businesses there can profit enough to make the effort worth while. As we have noted, the economic benefits of outdoor recreation are widely dispersed geographically; often only a small part are realized within or near the recreation area itself. Lastly, if successful businesses serving the relatively remote recreationist are to develop in a depressed area, it is highly doubtful if the residents of that area have the managerial skills, business experience, and capital to take advantage of those opportunities. They may, however, find employment in such businesses. While such employment is often seasonal and at wages that seem low by national standards, yet earnings of this kind may be higher than in marginal farming and certainly better than unemployment. The business itself will often be organized and conducted by a more experienced, better financed operator from some other city or locality.

POLICY ISSUES

The discussion and data presented in this chapter seem to raise some issues of public policy. How far should the public attempt to capture all or part of the values it creates? Establishment of a park, building of a new dam and reservoir with recreation potential, or constructing a new road to tap a hitherto relatively inaccessible area, all create economic values arising out of recreation. Public action creates these values; in the absence of specific public action, various private individuals will capture these values for their own. Some of the values will arise for land around the reservoir or other area, some will accrue to business establishments serving the recreationist—including business establishments in his home town and far from the scene of his outdoor recreation activities. Public actions in many fields create economic values which some private individuals capture, so outdoor recreation is not unique in this respect. Occasionally, some of these values are captured by direct public measures; more commonly, a part of them are captured through corporation and personal income taxes. Under the present federal tax programs in the United States, these methods do capture a significant part, though perhaps less than half, of any private profits arising out of public action.

Capture of private profits arising out of public action in the provision of outdoor recreation raises several questions of policy and of equity. In addition, it raises major questions of administrative practicality. If we decide to capture some of the benefits, how can we best do it? The people who use the outdoor recreation areas benefit, or else they would not come; some of their benefits could be captured by entrance fees or charges. This is a matter to which we shall return in more detail in Chapter VII. What about the benefits arising to the various businesses that supply the recreationists—the hotel and motel keepers, the service station operators, the restaurateurs, the sports shop owners, etc.? It might be possible to raise considerable revenue by taxes levied on such businesses or on some of the products sold by them. However, it would often be impossible to distinguish between the gasoline or the dinner bought by a recreationist and that bought by someone who neither uses nor wants to use the recreation area. The widely dispersed nature of the benefits should be recalled in this connection. The auto dealer in the distant city may benefit considerably from a new recreation development, for instance; yet, how to secure from him a contribution to the public purse equal to a part of the gain from the public expenditure, without creating hardship for those not gaining? We might conclude that the public benefit was so considerable, and so widely dispersed, that a general tax of some kind would be equitable as well as financially rewarding. For instance, some states have enacted small (1 cent per pack) taxes on cigarettes to help finance state parks; while not every smoker uses such areas, and while some users do not smoke, niceties of equity are subordinated to practicalities of revenue raising. Direct sales taxes on items which can be used only for outdoor recreation, such as guns or fishing tackle, are more commonly used.

There seem excellent arguments for imposition of general income taxes by states and sometimes even by local governments; and for use of some of the money so raised for outdoor recreation. If benefits are considerable but widely dispersed, a general income tax may capture more of them, from the beneficiaries only, than any other means. Provision of outdoor recreation certainly costs money and making most beneficiaries contribute to it in some proportion to their ability to pay seems equitable.

7

WHO PAYS AND HOW?

THE OPPORTUNITY TO ENJOY OUTDOOR RECREATION is never costless; while it may seem "free," this only means that the costs have been borne by someone else. The whole recreation experience obviously costs something to anyone who partakes of it (although costs for some user-oriented recreation may be very low indeed), if he but reflects a moment on the whole experience. But our concern in this chapter is with the recreation opportunity—the on-site experience—only. Society as a whole bears a cost in making such opportunities available; and this means that some individual or individuals have borne these costs, for society is made up of individuals. The cost may be so widely dispersed among many individuals that each is unaware of his share, but this does not abolish the costs. The person who actually enjoys the outdoor recreation experience may avoid any cost—perhaps none is levied on him— but this does not reduce the cost to zero, in the sense of the larger community.

At a much earlier time in our history, the costs of providing outdoor recreation opportunity were far less than today—and the values were far less, too. A person or a group could go into more or less natural surroundings, with virtually no capital improvements on them, and enjoy outdoor recreation. If it was hunting or fishing or camping, the natural unimproved qualities of the site could be used; water dipped from a stream or lake, with no thought and little danger of pollution, human wastes disposed of behind the nearest bushes, and in other respects, life in the raw. Or enterprising small boys could clear up a vacant lot or tract sufficiently to have a homemade baseball diamond or other playfield. The need and demand for land for other purposes was sufficiently low, and the intensity of the recreation use sufficiently low, that this kind of out-door recreation experience was possible without serious problems. The cost to society or to any individual from this sort of recreation, in any way, was small; the land had little alternative use value, and in any case other activities were not interfered with substantially.

All this has changed today, except in relatively few and remote locations; and the future will see even further change. Land, water, forests, and other natural resources used for outdoor recreation have, in general, substantial value for other purposes; to forgo the other uses means a cost for the whole society. Equally important, with the use intensities that are developing on nearly all outdoor recreation areas, substantial improvements are necessary; access roads must be built and maintained, safe drinking water supplies must be provided, wastes of all kinds must be disposed of (with consequent frequent servicing costs as well as investment), and various other services are usually necessary. All of this costs somebody some real money; a free entrance to the recreation area should not fool anyone that the rec-reation is in fact "free."

124

Provision of resource-based and intermediate public outdoor recreation opportunity in the United States, including the services necessary in the use and management of such areas, involves cash costs in the rough magnitude of $300 to $400 million annually. In addition, the governments forgo the opportunity for income from these areas that may amount to something of the same magnitude. Furthermore, user-oriented areas require substantial outlays. For a country with a gross national product in excess of $500 billion, these are not burdensome sums; but they are still important figures. Costs will surely rise in the future, as demand and use rise. It is possible that costs will not rise by ten times by 2000, even if demand increases by this amount. On the one hand, the increasing intensity of use of available areas may mean a less than proportionate increase in cost of areas; and it is probable that larger numbers can be accommodated and managed without proportionate increases. However, additions to present park systems will cost far more, proportionately, than did the establishment of the present parks. Whatever the future cost may be, it will surely be larger than the present cost—and large enough to present serious problems, if it is to be met and the needed areas provided.

The best means of financing outdoor recreation opportunity has had relatively little consideration in the past. The appeals for the appropriation of public funds have nearly always been on an emotional basis. This may have been wise from the viewpoint of those advocating more and better parks. The economics of outdoor recreation were imperfectly understood—still are—and it probably was easier to rally the necessary political support on an emotional rather than on a logical basis. But it is greatly to be doubted if this will be true in the future. The costs will be so much higher, especially in absolute terms but probably also relative to national income. Outdoor recreation will increasingly be forced to compete with the more commercial uses of the same natural resources. All of this will make the matter of payment for outdoor recreation opportunities more important and more a matter of public policy.

125

OUTDOOR RECREATION OPPORTUNITY
FROM GENERAL TAX REVENUES

A relatively simple procedure, governmentally speaking, is to appropriate from general tax revenues available to each level of government, such sums as are necessary to provide outdoor recreation to the desired level or to the level that can be afforded. Under this arrangement, taxes are raised in various ways, and paid into a common pool; and appropriations are made for various purposes, including provision of outdoor recreation opportunity, and paid from the same common pool (Figure 15). Total inflow must be as large

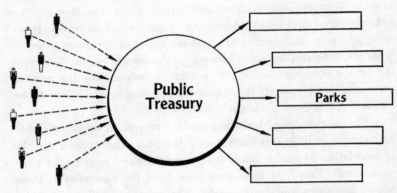

Figure 15. Schematic representation of payment of general taxes and support of parks out of general tax revenue.

as total outflow, at least over a period of time, although borrowings for capital improvements are not precluded. This is the basic method of government finance, one approved by the orthodox students and practitioners of government. Other means include special taxes tied to special uses; we shall discuss these later, as applied to outdoor recreation.

One major characteristic of this approach is that the level and sources of taxes are set separately, or largely so, from the level of expenditures for any particular purpose. No one can say, the taxes I pay go into this or that particular activity, for his taxes go into a common pool out of which all governmental costs are paid. Even the economist or other student of government finds it difficult to measure who pays for a particular type of governmental service—outdoor recreation, in our case. One can ascertain the present sources of governmental revenue—so much from general property taxes, so much from corporate income tax, so much from individual income tax, and so on. One may say, as a rough first approximation, that taxpayers share the costs of a particular government service in proportion as they share total tax payments. Thus, a city or county which relies heavily or exclusively on the general property tax for all its revenues is relying equally on this source for the taxes that support outdoor recreation. The federal government today raises most of its revenue from corporate and personal income taxes, and thus it may be said that its funds for outdoor recreation come from these sources.

This method of rough approximation may not be satisfactory when considerable changes in costs for a particular service are contemplated. If a unit of government at some level proposes to increase its expenditures on outdoor recreation substantially—enough that the increase cannot be absorbed out of present general revenues—then it must consider how it will raise the additional money. The question then becomes: what are the most probable sources of new tax revenue? The present source may be primarily general property tax, for example, but the new source may be entirely a personal income tax. If this be true, then one can say that costs of expanded outdoor recreation will be borne by those who pay the personal income tax. The reverse of this approach may also be used; one can say, if present costs for outdoor recreation were abolished, how might taxes be cut? The probable tax cuts would show who now bears the costs, under this approach.

Substantial segments, but not all, of a total population pay each kind of taxes, but not necessarily in the same proportions. Property taxes fall, at first hand, on property owners, and secondarily on tenants; they are frequently not in proportion to incomes of persons, and thus not in proportion to ability to pay. Income taxes typically allow exemptions for certain minimum amounts of income and for dependents, and are also often graduated upward with income; thus they are "progressive," in the economist's sense of the word. Sales or excise taxes typically are levied according to expenditures made; they fall more heavily on income groups making the kinds of expenditures on which taxes are levied than they do on other groups.

The basic characteristic of financing outdoor recreation out of general tax revenues is that use and enjoyment of the recreation opportunity so provided are not directly related to payment of taxes; and indirectly may be in far different proportions. Payment of costs and realization of benefits are so separated that many, perhaps most, citizens do not connect them at all.

OBJECTIONS TO USE OF GENERAL TAX REVENUES

Various objections, on different and not necessarily logically consistent grounds, can be made to sole or major reliance on general tax revenues as a source of financial support for provision of outdoor recreation opportunity. Let us examine the major objections, one by one, recognizing that more than one ground for objection is possible and that the various grounds are not necessarily logical.

One basic objection is that many users of outdoor recreation areas and facilities reside and pay taxes in units of government other than the one which provides the recreation opportunity. This is perhaps most marked at the level of state parks; substantial proportions—over half for some states and far larger for some parks—of all use is by nonresidents of the state. The same situation is true, to a lesser extent, for county and city parks; some users come from other counties and cities. It is also true to a limited degree for federal outdoor recreation areas; some users come from other countries. When use is by persons from other governmental jurisdictions, these users cannot contribute, through general tax revenues, to the costs of such recreation opportunity, if the latter are borne out of general tax revenues. One group is asked to pay taxes to provide outdoor recreation for another group. It may be argued that businesses in the home state or area benefit from money brought in by outsiders; based upon our earlier analysis, it seems probable that the extent of this business benefit will be less than the costs directly incurred in provision of the recreation opportunity. With the increasing population mobility, due in part to the better transportation, this problem will increase in importance over the next several decades.

A second objection to payment of costs of providing outdoor recreation opportunity from general tax revenues is that many taxpayers do not use the outdoor recreation facilities so provided. This type of objection was once advanced against universal free public education; more than a hundred years ago Herbert Spencer, for instance, thought it was immoral to force one man to pay for the education of another man's children. Still later, the same argument was used against public health services. In these two cases, the total electorate has long since decided that the general public benefits of a minimum literacy and a minimum level of health were so great as to far outweigh any inequities that arise out of using general tax revenues for these purposes. There are still some diehards even here, of course; the author was astonished to discover a couple of years ago a man who seriously proposed abolishing public schools and making education the responsibility of "free private enterprise"; and there has recently been notable resistance to extensions of publicly supported health services. But education and health are widely accepted in this role; so has been outdoor recreation on a modest or low level of expenditures in the past. It is, however, extremely doubtful if this general public acceptance of using total tax revenues to provide outdoor recreation to a part of the total population extends to the vastly larger expenditures that will be required in the years ahead, if demands are to be met.

A closely related argument is that, as a matter of equity, those enjoying outdoor recreation provided at public expense should be required to pay for it, more or less proportionately to their use. This

129

argument rests upon the general fairness of their doing so. It can be, and often is, buttressed these days by pointing out that those using outdoor recreation can afford to pay the costs involved. The rising demand for outdoor recreation, which necessitates increases in public expenditures to provide it, comes in large part from higher average per capita incomes. People can afford the other costs involved in the total or whole recreation experience—at least, they make them. If they can afford these costs, so the argument goes—costs which are generally far larger than any reasonable cost for the recreation opportunity itself—then they should be able to bear the latter costs

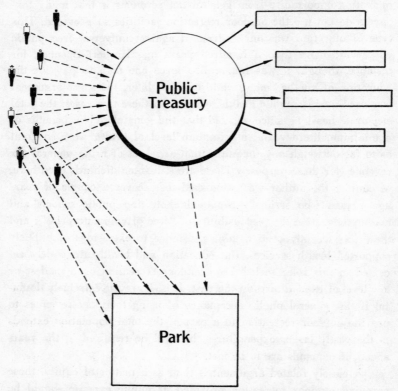

Figure 16. When parks are financed by user charges, general taxes need not be used for park management, or at least not to the same degree.

as well. As we have noted in earlier chapters, there is much validity to this latter point.

Another argument against provision of outdoor recreation opportunity from general tax revenues is a more practical or expedient one: that legislative bodies will be unwilling to vote the sums needed to provide outdoor recreation opportunity to meet future demands, if the money must come from the general tax revenues. Many other costs of government at all levels are rising, and competition for the tax dollar increases. There is also a major tendency for expenditures to reflect past patterns of demand; changes come slowly and only under continued pressure. If total or major reliance is placed upon general tax revenues to provide outdoor recreation opportunity, then it is highly probable that expenditures will lag seriously behind need. In the end, of course, this may save little, since future costs of acquiring areas may be much higher than present costs.

ROLE OF USER CHARGES

The foregoing objections to the use of general tax revenues to provide outdoor recreation opportunity have led to increased attention to user charges levied on recreationists. One possible means of financing all or part of the current management costs or of the capital investment costs, or both, required to provide the vastly increased range of outdoor recreation opportunity likely to be demanded in the future is the imposition of charges against the users of such areas (Figure 16).

The arguments in favor of higher user charges are largely the reverse of the objections to the use of general tax revenues. That is, by means of user charges persons not resident in the governmental unit that provides the outdoor recreation opportunity can be made to pay part or all the costs involved. Out of state, out of county, or out of city residents can thus contribute their share, or part of it, to the costs. Those people who use outdoor recreation areas, whether resident within the governmental unit or not, can pay part,

131

most, or all of the costs; and those people who do not use such facilities are not expected to pay for them, or at least not as much. This would solve the equity problem of one group using facilities provided by another group. Finally, and in highly practical political terms, it may be only through user charges that sufficient public revenue can be raised to pay for the necessary areas and facilities. It is noteworthy that several states have turned to user charges as one source of finance, especially when appropriations have lagged seriously; and that some groups once adamant against user charges have reluctantly accepted them as necessary.

Major reliance upon user charges to finance outdoor recreation opportunity makes it clear that government (at any level) often operates in two separate capacities, which are frequently confused. On the one hand, it is an entrepreneur—an arranger, a planner, a builder, an operator. In this role, it has some similarities with private entrepreneurship; however, government (at some level) may often undertake services which have little or no prospect of profit; they may be highly appropriate for government, because of their value to its citizens. On the other hand, government (at some level) is often called upon as a financier—to pay, out of its general revenues, for the services it provides. The two roles are separable; government may undertake the first but refuse the second. This seems to be evolving in outdoor recreation, and it is entirely possible that it will become vastly more important in the future.

Imposition of user charges to pay all or a substantial part of the costs of providing outdoor recreation opportunity does not preclude the use of governmental credit to borrow investment funds, which are later repaid out of the revenues. In fact, this combination has been resorted to in several states or cities, and has been proposed at the federal level. An investment fund, large enough to acquire substantial areas in relation to the need for them, is established, by borrowings or from general public funds on hand; and this sum is repaid, with or without interest, over a period of years from revenues obtained from user charges. This type of public financial operation is closely akin to common business practice; bonds or other debt instruments are used to raise funds now, to be repaid later from income arising out of the investment. By immediate or early acquisition of areas, public interest in and support of the program may be assured, and as a result there may be a far greater willingness to pay entrance fees or other charges for use of the recreation areas.

Entrance fees or other charges could be, but generally have not been, used as a deliberate management tool in recreation areas. The *way* in which fees or charges are levied may be as important as their amount. For instance, fees might be levied only on days or hours of heavy use; this would both reduce the costs of collection (which are sometimes high relative to the money collected) and also would provide an incentive for users to shift use to hours and days when use would otherwise be less than capacity. Entrance fees might be levied on a per car basis or on a per person basis; the first would provide substantial relief to large families. Charges might be levied on a per visit basis, or for a limited number of days (perhaps a week or two), or for a season, for instance. Season-long charges in effect mean a zero charge after the first visit; they would tend to keep out the casual visitor much more than the heavy user. Many other possible methods can be devised; each would have its particular effect upon attendance by different groups.

A related question is: what effect would entrance fees above a token level have upon the kind of use made of an outdoor recreation area? For one thing, it probably would discourage the mere curiosity seeker; the party who now drives through a national park because the scenery is "pretty" probably would not do so if the entrance fee were $10 or $20, for instance. This effect would probably be large in the national parks and national forests. Would people use outdoor recreation areas with better manners and more respect if they had to pay a higher fee for them? Do nearly zero fees encourage people to treat areas as nearly worthless? We all know that people tend to waste water when it is not metered, or other services when a flat charge is made. Vandalism, carelessness with litter, and other problems arising from a public that sometimes does not seem to value recreation resources highly plague all or most

133

recreation management agencies. Possibly higher fees, especially if coupled with better services, would lead to a much better use of the area. It is, of course, possible that higher entrance fees would have the opposite effect; people might feel that paying fees gave them a right to throw their litter where they chose.

Various arguments have been or may be advanced against the use of user charges, especially against charges significantly higher than at present. On the one hand, it is argued that entrance fees would keep poor people out of parks, and that these are the people who need them most. This argument has considerable validity if it is proposed to levy entrance charges on user-oriented areas; but it has almost no validity if applied to intermediate and resource-based areas. The other costs of visiting the latter are so large, relevant to any entrance fees that are likely to be levied, as to render this argument invalid. As we have noted in earlier chapters, the truly poor people unfortunately never get to these types of parks in any case. An entirely different kind of argument against levying substantial entrance charges to recreation areas is that it is administratively infeasible to collect them—that it will cost more than can be collected. This argument also has validity in many situations. The typical city park is freely open, all around, to visitors; they do not usually go through a gate or other control point; the area is open to use throughout the whole day. Under these circumstances, it would indeed be very difficult to collect an entrance charge. A different situation exists for many more remote parks, where use most of the time is so low that it would cost as much to collect a fee as could be collected. However, the Forest Service and some state park systems are experimenting with "do-it-yourself" fee-paying devices. Most people want to pay their way, and there is a large willingness to meet reasonable costs; this can be supplemented by spot checks and enforcement. A great many state parks, national forests, national parks, and other areas lie in such a way, or entrance roads have been constructed in such a way, that entry is in fact largely restricted to a very few points. Where this is true, and where usage passes some minimum point at some times, fee collection would seem entirely practical, administratively speaking. It would probably be undesirable to try to collect enough fees to meet costs in each park in a system; instead, the system as a whole should be considered, with higher earnings on some units offsetting lower earnings on others.

A third major kind of argument against user charges for outdoor recreation is a more emotional or intuitive one. Some people say: provision of outdoor recreation opportunity is a proper public activity, like provision of public schools, and it is simply wrong to charge for it. This argument runs head on into the arguments against use of general tax revenues for this purpose. Being intuitive and emotional, it can often not be met with fact and logic; the practical necessity of other sources of revenues may be more decisive. The situation is not unlike that faced in school desegregation in the South: do you prefer integrated schools to no schools at all? Do you prefer public parks available at a user charge or do you prefer public parks so hopelessly overcrowded as in fact to be unavailable?

Attitudes toward user charges may depend in large part upon the way in which charges are levied, or upon the services charged for. Many people would accept charges for special services, such as boat launching ramps, who would greatly oppose general park entrance charges, for instance. Charges might be made for parking rather than for entrance; additional charges for camping may be more acceptable than entrance fees. Many people feel that historic sites and some nationally famous spots are part of the national heritage, for which it is wrong to charge admission. They might not feel this way about entrance fees to more ordinary recreation areas.

The attitude of the public toward paying fees for outdoor recreation areas will depend largely upon how well the rationale for fees has been explained to them. If they understand, they will oppose less.

GRANTS-IN-AID FOR
OUTDOOR RECREATION

A different way of meeting the problem of one unit of government providing outdoor recreation opportunity which is used by citizens of other units of government is the use of grants-in-aid. These grants may be from the federal government to states, counties, and cities; or from states to counties and cities. Each is in use or proposed. One key recommendation of the Outdoor Recreation Commission was for federal grants-in-aid to states, for two purposes: first, as a stimulus to state-wide recreation planning; and second, as a help in buying needed additional areas. The federal housing program, as we have noted, includes grants from the federal government for the acquisition of open space land in urbanized areas. Some of the states, such as New York, New Jersey, Pennsylvania, Wisconsin, and California, either have made or propose to make grants-in-aid to counties and cities, primarily to acquire needed land.

Grants-in-aid go a long way to meet the argument that many users come from outside the taxing area of the government providing the recreation area. By widening the taxing area, it and the use area may be brought more nearly into agreement. Grants-in-aid may reduce opposition to use of tax revenues for provision of outdoor recreation, by making the tax burden less direct and less obvious; but this is mere conjecture, since there is insufficient experience to be sure. On the other hand, grants-in-aid do not meet the objection that only some taxpayers use outdoor recreation areas, nor do they meet the equity argument advanced against use of general tax revenues.

Grants-in-aid from one level of government to lower levels usually have the important advantage of spurring the latter into taking actions which otherwise would be long delayed. In our American system of government, we bitterly oppose efforts of higher levels of government to compel lower units to do what the latter do not wish to do. But we are often willing to establish grants or other assistance, to help those lower units of government which want to do something but lack the initiative or the means. In time, the less enthusiastic areas often see the advantages and accept grants or help also. This approach has been used in many fields—agriculture, highways, health, air transport, and many others. As we noted in Chapter II, this was critical in the development of state park systems in the 1930's. A state or county that is reluctant to provide outdoor recreation opportunity for its own citizens and positively hostile to the idea of providing it for citizens of other states or counties, may be moved to act if part of the costs are paid by the federal government.

Possibly even more important than *whether* is *how*, as far as grants from federal and state levels to lower levels are concerned. Grants for planning, either complete or on a matching basis, would greatly stimulate planning at the lower levels, and in the end almost certainly result in major savings. Grants for land acquisition in advance of critical need would certainly save money and, perhaps more important, fuss and bother. Land for public purposes can often be bought easily and cheaply if bought soon enough; later, it is not only more costly but its purchase stirs up far more opposition. Questions may well be raised as to whether the grant should be an outright gift of part of the purchase cost, or a heavily subsidized loan which would later be repaid. Over the past few decades this country has evolved the "nonrecourse" loan in agriculture; a farmer pledges his wheat, corn, or cotton, often at the full market price; he receives an interest-free loan; if the price moves up, he pays off the loan and pockets the gain; if the price moves down, he forfeits the commodities and the debt is cancelled. Why could not something like this be extended to outdoor recreation? The federal government or a state might establish a recreation loan fund; lower units of government could borrow 100 per cent of the cost of land to buy additional areas of land, subject to review of its land appraisal procedures and perhaps subject to the requirement that the areas so bought would fit into a long-term recreation plan; the land itself would be the complete security for the loan; when the lower level of government moved to develop the tract, it would pay off the loan, and go ahead. If it never developed the land, the latter could revert to the lender as full satisfaction for the loan. This procedure might be tied to an interest-free loan period, such as we now provide for federal irrigation development. These and perhaps other arrangements would make it possible for local government to buy land well in advance of urgent need.

One important aspect of grants-in-aid is a negative one: avoid providing an incentive to the recipient to avoid doing what it should do, or to pass the full burden back to you. That is, grants should be carefully devised to encourage recipients to undertake their own actions along desired lines, not to move in opposite directions.

POLICY ISSUES

The discussion in this chapter seems to raise a number of policy issues, where the answers are not obvious.

First of all, how do we as a nation wish to regard provision of outdoor recreation opportunity: as a general public service, to be paid for by everyone regardless of their personal participation? Or as a special and extra service, for those sectors of the total population that want it, but that should also largely pay for it? Stated in this way, the issue seems general and possibly remote to many people. But the answer will determine our specific policies on many issues.

For instance, what is the most equitable way to pay for outdoor recreation opportunity? If we regard it as a general public service, in the same sense as schools, then the needed funds should be raised from as broad a tax base as possible. If we regard it as a more special service, for part of the population only (a self-nominated part), then costs should be levied primarily against users. This leads to a more specific question: how high should user charges be, and on what basis should they be levied? If we regard provision of outdoor recreation as something of a special service for only that part of the population which seems to want it, and if we separate the role of government into the entrepreneurial and financial parts, then we can well argue for meeting a substantial part of recreation costs out of user charges. If we resort to such charges, should they pay part or all of the annual operating costs, or should they be used primarily or exclusively to buy additional lands, or does it matter how they are used? If we propose to employ user charges to a major extent, does it matter whether the revenue so raised is directly plowed back into recreation, rather than go to general tax revenues and be appropriated for recreation (and maybe some get lost along the way)? Should we consciously and deliberately use user charges as a management tool, to encourage or direct use to areas, times, and ways we think desirable?

Should the nation use grants-in-aid for outdoor recreation extensively? Are not, or might not, such grants be merely a way of evading opposition to their purpose, and doing indirectly what there is insufficient popular support to do directly? Should the granting level of government spell out rather carefully the uses to which grant funds can be put, and specify conditions under which grant money can be used, or should the grants merely be general financial aid from one level of government to another?

Lastly, how can we lift the discussion and consideration of methods of financing to a higher plane than a mere consideration of who pays? That is, are the problems of adequate finance central to all future recreation progress? If so, must we not think in broader terms than merely to consider on whom the burden falls? Must we not also consider the relation between method of financing and the amount of money the public is willing to put into this activity?

Throughout this chapter, we have treated expenditures out of general tax revenues, fee charges, and grants-in-aid as alternative measures. In fact, however, they could be supplementary, to a large degree. The issue need not be one versus the other, but how much of one versus how much of another. Innumerable mixtures are possible in practice.

8

WHAT OF THE FUTURE?

LET US LOOK MORE EXPLICITLY, IN SUMMARY fashion, at some of the probable changes the future will bring for outdoor recreation, and at some of the policy issues these will raise.

Dominating the outlook for the future is the probability—one may almost say the certainty—of a vastly increased demand for outdoor recreation. All the components of that demand are trending upward: population is increasing at about 1.7 per cent per year; per capita real income is rising at about the same average rate; some groups in the population are getting a lot more leisure and most people are getting a little more of it; and transportation facilities are improving steadily, permitting faster movement over longer distances. In the past, the combined effect of these forces has led to an increase in outdoor recreation of about 10 per cent per year. This may not sound high, but two comparisons may help: first, this means a doubling in attendance every eight years; and second, very few economic series show any faster growth rate. No one knows or can know just how fast and how far total recreation demand will rise in the future. The author has estimated that total recreation use in 2000 will be ten times what it was in 1956; it has already nearly doubled since 1956, so the increase by 2000 will be nearer five times the present. The Outdoor Recreation Resources Review Commission, using essentially the same data, estimated that it would treble between 1960 and 2000. At the present stage of our knowledge, it is impossible to prove that either is right or that either is wrong; only time will tell. No informed observer that we know of has suggested demand will remain at the present level or decline. The only differences of opinion are as to the extent and rapidity of the rise.

If demand rises greatly, the area required for outdoor recreation will certainly increase also. An increase in area proportional to the increase in demand is probably impossible of achievement, perhaps even unnecessary. The nation can, however, afford the land and water resources demanded for outdoor recreation. We have a surplus of cropland acreage now and are expected to continue to have one for the next several decades. Much of our large forested area is usable for outdoor recreation, to a greater extent than at present. Much land, not highly valued or urgently needed for agriculture or forestry, could be made into parks to provide satisfactory outdoor recreation on a mass basis. While water supplies are limited in some regions, for much of the country there is enough water to devote a lot more to recreation use. The United States is *not* pinched for natural resources; we can use much larger amounts for outdoor recreation in the future than we have in the past.

Although recreation area is almost sure to expand in the future, the intensity of use of most recreation areas will rise. More people on a given area of land or water: is this crowding? The answer depends partly on how many more people, and partly by what you mean by "crowding." The latter is largely a psychological concept; what is crowding to me may not be to you, or vice versa. While some kinds of past uses may be somewhat hampered by many more people per unit of area, yet there exist great possibilities for more use without serious restraint. We have noted that many areas are unused or used very lightly a large part of the time; by spreading some of the use to such periods, crowding may be avoided. Large parts of many present areas are very lightly used; they could be brought into more active use. Skillful design and management can often get more people on the same gross area without people being generally aware of heavier use. We may have to learn to accept more people, and closer proximity to other people, as part of the great outdoors.

The costs of providing this larger area, of developing it, and of providing for the visitors will certainly be much higher than in the past—it may well be higher per unit of use. The increases in numbers of people and in area would in themselves result in much higher costs. In the past, a lot of the outdoor recreation took place more or less incidentally to general land management. This was especially marked in the case of the national forests, but it was true on other kinds of areas also. In the future, outdoor recreation use will almost surely be at such a high level as to require substantially more administrative expenditures. The nation can afford whatever these costs may be. Higher incomes will be one basic factor underlying the higher use which leads to the higher cost; the higher incomes can provide the wherewithal to meet those costs. There may be difficult problems in *how* to raise the needed funds; there need be no question about the nation's ability to pay for the services demanded.

MAJOR POLICY ISSUES
FOR THE FUTURE

Let us briefly recapitulate and re-emphasize the major policy issues likely to arise in the future, as far as outdoor recreation is concerned.

First of all, how may we, as a nation, plan better for our outdoor recreation needs? We have noted the wide diversity of public agencies and private groups providing outdoor recreation. How can their planning be coordinated without being centralized (which we assume few would want to see)? A closely related problem is: how can we estimate with more confidence the future demands for outdoor recreation, so that we shall neither neglect to provide what is needed nor make unnecessarily large expenditures? As we have noted, the present basis for making such estimates of future demand is weak. Research might help to provide some answers to the latter question. The federal government has recently taken some steps that may help with the coordination problem, but it probably will remain a subject for continuing public attention at all levels of government.

Secondly, *how* can we best finance the expected greater costs for outdoor recreation in the future? How much shall we rely on general taxes, how much on special taxes earmarked for this purpose, how much upon user charges? Shall we try to raise the necessary money entirely in the unit of local government in which the recreation area lies, or shall we resort to large-scale grants-in-aid, from the federal government to states and local government and from states to the latter? We have noted that the nation can afford the money; but how to raise it is not so simple.

Thirdly, what are the most appropriate relations between governments, federal, state, and local, in this matter of providing outdoor recreation? While there is some differentiation of activity according to level of government, it is far from complete. Cities do not operate national parks, it is true; but state and federal agencies operate areas very similar to city parks. Might it be possible to get a somewhat cleaner division between different kinds of government, as to their functions? Could we more sharply distinguish between planning and perhaps financing, which may have to be done on a broader scale, from operation of recreation areas, which perhaps can be more localized?

Fourthly, how can we best reserve needed outdoor recreation areas at the most appropriate time? This is especially serious in expanding suburbs; if needed land is not reserved at the right time, it is built upon and to all intents and purposes is permanently lost to recreation. Money cost is less if land is bought early; "turmoil" cost, or opposition to public acquisition, particularly is lower at an early date than later. But it is often hard to rally popular support to expenditure of public funds for a future rather than for a present need. Is the answer some kind of public land reserve, or a public bank to finance land purchases for future need? How can we best devise a new instrument or method of dealing with this problem?

Lastly, how may we best raise the quality of the outdoor recreation experience for the average user? In asking this question, we are fully aware that "quality" is hard to define and may depend upon subjective value standards. Yet almost everyone would agree that some kinds of experiences are more meaningful than others, that some people seem to get more from outdoor recreation than do others. In our preoccupation with numbers of visitors, there may be a danger that we neglect the quality dimension of their experience. In publicly provided outdoor recreation opportunity, the public agencies cannot escape the responsibility for the quality of the experience, for their actions largely determine it. Could we, by more explicitly facing the problem, do a better job in the future than in the past?

These policy issues are primarily economic, social, governmental, not technological nor concerning resource availability. Some of the latter kinds of problems do indeed exist, but in our judgment they are not the critical ones. These human problems partly grow out of the changing volume and nature of the outdoor recreation demand; they also arise in part because they have had little attention in the past. Such issues, when they have arisen, have tended to be debated on an emotional and preconceptual basis; social science research has generally not been brought to bear upon their solution. It could be; this may be the real challenge for young people entering this field today.

PRINTED IN U.S.A.